CW00541936

Bullying Interventio

Bullying Interventions in Schools

Six Basic Approaches

Ken Rigby

A John Wiley & Sons, Ltd., Publication

This Wiley-Blackwell edition published 2012

Text © Ken Rigby 2010

First published 2010 in Australia and New Zealand only by ACER Press, an imprint of Australian Council *for* Educational Research Ltd

Wiley-Blackwell is an imprint of John Wiley & Sons, formed by the merger of Wiley's global Scientific, Technical and Medical business with Blackwell Publishing.

Registered Office
John Wiley & Sons Ltd, The Atrium, Southern Gate, Chichester, West Sussex, PO19 8SQ, UK

Editorial Offices
350 Main Street, Malden, MA 02148-5020, USA
9600 Garsington Road, Oxford, OX4 2DQ, UK
The Atrium, Southern Gate, Chichester, West Sussex, PO19 8SQ, UK

For details of our global editorial offices, for customer services, and for information about how to apply for permission to reuse the copyright material in this book please see our website at www.wiley.com/wiley-blackwell.

The right of Ken Rigby to be identified as the author of this work has been asserted in accordance with the UK Copyright, Designs and Patents Act 1988.

All rights reserved. No part of this publication may be reproduced, stored in a retrieval system, or transmitted, in any form or by any means, electronic, mechanical, photocopying, recording or otherwise, except as permitted by the UK Copyright, Designs and Patents Act 1988, without the prior permission of the publisher.

Wiley also publishes its books in a variety of electronic formats. Some content that appears in print may not be available in electronic books.

Designations used by companies to distinguish their products are often claimed as trademarks. All brand names and product names used in this book are trade names, service marks, trademarks or registered trademarks of their respective owners. The publisher is not associated with any product or vendor mentioned in this book. This publication is designed to provide accurate and authoritative information in regard to the subject matter covered. It is sold on the understanding that the publisher is not engaged in rendering professional services. If professional advice or other expert assistance is required, the services of a competent professional should be sought.

Library of Congress Cataloging-in-Publication Data

Rigby, Ken.
Bullying interventions in schools : six basic approaches / Ken Rigby.
    p. cm.
    Includes bibliographical references and index.
    ISBN 978-1-118-34588-7 (cloth) – ISBN 978-1-118-34589-4 (pbk.)
1. Bullying in schools–Prevention.   I. Title.
    LB3013.3.R59 2012
    371.5′8–dc23

                                                        2012015986

A catalogue record for this book is available from the British Library.

Cover image: © Toby Maudsley / Getty Images.
Cover design by Cyan Design.

Set in 10.5/13pt Minion by SPi Publisher Services, Pondicherry, India
Printed in Singapore by Ho Printing Singapore Pte Ltd

1   2012

Contents

Foreword

Dr Ken Rigby's work is at the vanguard of the leadership South Australia has taken to address bullying and has been established on a foundation of research that seeks sound evidence and best practice.

Indeed, for decades Dr Rigby has been an internationally renowned leader in this area. He brings clarity, intellect, and rigor to the assessment of research and evidence and acknowledges there are no magic solutions.

Our South Australian community has sought to work together to support young people in our schools. For example, our Coalition to decrease bullying, harassment, and violence, which includes Dr Ken Rigby as an inaugural member, brings together the three schooling sectors and eminent researchers to provide expert advice to our education sector. Increased awareness of bullying has led to school communities becoming better informed as policies, subsequent training, and more effective responses have been developed.

This book adds to our store of knowledge and practical approaches, based on Dr Rigby's acknowledged wealth of research and experience. He helps practitioners and parents alike by virtue of his accessible and lucid presentation of the facts and research.

I trust this book will further assist and inform school leaders, teachers, and counselors as they work to overcome bullying and create a safe and supportive learning environment.

The Hon. Dr Jane Lomax-Smith MP Minister for Education,
South Australia

Acknowledgments

I would like to thank the following:

The South Australian Department of Education and Children's Services (DECS) and the committee members of the Coalition to Decrease Bullying, Harassment and Violence in South Australian schools, for their encouragement and support in enabling some of the content of this book to be piloted with teachers in workshops attended by staff members from the State, Catholic, and Independent sectors.

Greg Cox, Policy Advisor, Student Behaviour Management, School & District Operations in South Australia, for his constant support in publicizing and promoting this work.

Jacqueline Van Velsen, Education Officer – Youth Services, Catholic Education, Ballarat for her practical help, advice, and encouragement.

Bob Bellhouse, writer, editor, and founder of Inyahead Press for his valuable practical advice.

Sheri Bauman, Associate Professor at the University of Arizona, for her fine work in researching with me on how teachers and counselors handle cases of bullying in schools internationally.

Colleen McCloughlin, Senior Lecturer in Education at the University of Cambridge, for providing the opportunity to make presentations and provide workshops in which ideas relating to this book were discussed.

Curriculum Corporation (see www.curriculum.edu.au), for granting permission for the use of the illustration on mediation that appears in *Hidden Hurt* by Lewers and Murphy (2000, p. 61).

Practice from <www.restorativejustice.org.uk>.

Daniel Goleman, for permission to reproduce a case study illustrating 'social intelligence' published in *Greater Good*, Volume 111, Issue 2, Fall/Winter, 2006–2007, p. 44.

Introduction

After many years of neglect, there has recently been a flood of articles and books on bullying in schools. This is to be welcomed in that it recognizes the importance of this topic, not merely from an academic perspective but also from a social and humane point of view. It is difficult – if not impossible – to assess the amount of serious harm that is being done daily to millions of children throughout the world who are continually being victimized by their peers at school. But we do know that the effects of bullying are enormously damaging to the physical and mental health of many of these children and that the effects can persist into adult years.[1] Many people never recover from the bullying they experience at school.

There is no doubt that those concerned with the education of students are now much more aware of the situation than was the case some 30 or 40 years ago. As a school teacher in several schools in Australia in the 1960s, I cannot recall a single occasion on which the subject of school bullying was ever discussed among the staff. Of course, it was known to exist, as we knew from our own school days. But it was simply not a matter which anyone thought should be addressed. In most countries, it was not until the 1990s that schools began to take bullying seriously. Even then there were schools – and even Departments of Education – that were reluctant to acknowledge the problem and take systematic action. First slowly and then at an accelerating rate, measures were proposed, intervention programs were devised, and schools began to implement so-called anti-bullying policies. In many countries, such as Australia and Britain and in some states in the United States, it became mandatory to have such a written policy or plan describing what each school had agreed to do.

Over the last 10 years or so, we have entered a phase in which researchers have begun to ask whether the increased focus on school bullying has made any difference. Longitudinal studies have suggested that in many countries progress has been made, albeit small. In an examination of trends in levels of peer victimization in North America and Europe, significant reductions in reported peer victimization were indicated in 19 of the 27 schools from which data were obtained between 1997 and 2006.[2] The researchers point out, however, that the problem still remains a very serious one. A third of all the children in the overall sample reported occasional bullying or victimization and around 1 in 10 children reported chronic involvement, either as perpetrator or victim.

The study cited above suggests that the measures being taken to reduce bullying in schools have not yet proved to be very effective. This suggestion has been strongly supported by an increasing number of studies undertaken over the last five years that have sought to determine just how effective a range of interventive strategies have been in addressing the problem of school bullying.[3] These reports make sobering reading. Some researchers have reported that on average the numerous interventions have been ineffective; others point to small reductions of not more than 20 percent. In practical terms, this implies that if there are 10 cases of bullying taking place in a school, after the application of an anti-bullying program, one might expect 8 cases to be continuing! It is nevertheless true that in some schools anti-bullying programs have been much more effective than average, especially when programs have been implemented thoroughly. This provides us with some hope that a higher level of success can be achieved. But there is certainly a long way to go before most schools can confidently expect to eradicate most of the bullying that is going on.

In general, efforts to reduce bullying in schools have involved two complementary approaches. One is to direct attention to improving the attitudes and interpersonal behavior of *all* children in a school. This has been called the universal approach. Its aim is to prevent cases of bullying from ever occurring. It is thought that this may be done by educational means, for example, by educating students about the nature and harmfulness of bullying and promoting pro-social attitudes and the development of social skills that will result in positive inter-personal relations among all students.[4] To this end, appropriate curricula and teaching methods may be designed and applied to help children to interact more cooperatively and to respond more empath-ically to the distress experienced by others. One important development has been the use of 'circle time' in schools, which enables students to share their experiences and problems at school in a safe and struc-tured classroom environment.[5] Peer support programs may also be devised to enable interested students to help and support students experiencing difficulties with others, for instance, by intervening as bystanders when bullying takes place and providing psychological support for those victimized. Sometimes attempts to reduce bullying have been focused on improved classroom management and better engagement with students.[6] With improvements in the school ethos, we might expect bullying to become less common.

The second approach is to focus especially on the students who have become involved in bully/victim problems at school. The aim here is to stop the bullying from continuing and (sometimes) to help those who bully or have been victimized to lead more constructive or less troubled lives. Rather than direct attention to all the students in a school as occurs in the universal approach, this approach is selective in identifying those students who need specialized attention. A range of methods have been devised for this purpose. These form the main focus in this book and will be examined in detail later.

As noted above, these two approaches should be regarded as complementary. If the universal approach is successful, there will be fewer cases of bullying that need to be addressed. If the case-focused approach is successful, the task of bringing about positive changes in the total school ethos will be easier to accomplish. The relationship between the two may indeed be reciprocal: the more successful one of these approaches turns out to be, the less will be the need for the other.

There remains, however, the practical question of how much emphasis should be placed on each of these two approaches. It is easy to see that an emphasis on one approach to the exclusion of the other will simply not do. We would have to be exceedingly optimistic to believe that a program of prevention can be devised and implemented in schools to guarantee that no one will ever bully anyone. Surprisingly, there have been claims to this effect. One book title suggests that you can 'bully proof your school'; another, if you are a parent, that you can 'bully proof your child'.[7] I think we can discount such thinking as utopian. Equally, it would be foolish to suggest that we must rely entirely on waiting until bullying has occurred before we act. Children who bully are clearly influenced by the attitudes of those around them at school. We should not neglect the opportunity to inform all children about their social obligations and seek to promote ways in which they can relate to each other more positively. Moral and social education should form a part of every curriculum.

It is the 'universal approach' that currently dominates thinking about bullying. For some it is almost synonymous with the 'whole school approach'. Emphasis upon improving intervention methods to address actual cases of bullying is being described by many as 'reactive'. It is seen as closing the stable door after the horse has bolted. Recently, I gave a presentation on bullying to business managers in which I argued that preventative methods and interventive methods were both needed in tackling bullying in schools and the workplace. I was predictably told that I was being too reactive. Often now the universal approach is conceived as the basic approach. It is argued that every child is capable of engaging in bullying and every child should therefore be educated to engage in cooperative and helpful behavior among peers. Such social education should therefore be directed equally at all members of the school community. With enlightened educational practice – so it is maintained – the school ethos will be transformed and there will be no more bullying.

In studies of school bullying, the emerging orthodoxy can be summed up by a claim that is repeatedly being made in books and journals. It is that interventions that focus on the entire school population are more *effective* in reducing the bully/victim problem than interventions that focus on individual students.[8] This proposition to my knowledge has never been tested. Unfortunately, it has the effect of detracting from, or stifling developments in, work that is desperately needed to help individual children who are involved in serious bully/victim problems with their peers and see no end to the torment that they are experiencing.

What is needed, in my opinion, is a better balance between the universal and the more individualistic interventionist approaches. In this book, I want to correct or redress what I see as an overemphasis on the preventative and holistic approach to school bullying *at the expense of dealing with actual incidents of bullying*. I want to focus more on what schools can do when cases arise.

My reasons for believing that much more attention needs to be given to how to intervene in cases of bullying are as follows.

First of all, as numerous surveys have shown, there exists a relatively small proportion of students who are directly involved in a very high proportion of the cases of bullying that occur in a school. Although the interpersonal behavior of these students is affected by the general ethos of a school, their involvement in bullying is, to a considerable extent, determined by a range of factors that are *not* closely associated with what happens at school. These include predisposing personality factors and personal vulnerabilities which have their origin in genetic or biological influences, as well as environmental pressures from outside the school, most obviously through negative experiences of family life, beginning from early childhood. Whether the school environment contributes to the problem of bullying or helps to ameliorate the problem, schools are called upon to deal with these difficult cases. They constitute a high priority.

Parents – especially of those children who are bullied repeatedly at school – expect cases of bullying to be dealt with effectively. They are frequently disappointed. This was brought home to me several years ago when I received a large number of e-mails and letters from parents, many of them angry, miserable, and depressed, complaining bitterly of the failure of schools to help their children to be free from bullying.[9] Parents urgently want the problem relating to their child to be dealt with now and are not inclined to think that conditions will be created in the school that will make any intervention unnecessary.

Actual interventions that are undertaken by schools in cases of bullying that come to their attention are often unsuccessful. The low proportion of students who actually go to teachers requesting help to stop them being bullied (around 30 percent) commonly report that the situation does not improve.[10] Arguably, the students who are being bullied are the best judges of the effectiveness of teacher interventions.

Teachers typically are uncertain about how they can best deal with cases of bullying. This has become evident in surveys sampling the responses of teachers and counselors in different countries to questions about what they think they would do in cases of bullying.[11] This is not to blame school personnel. As we will see, knowing how to act so as to solve bully/victim problems is often problematic, and teachers are often not aware of what can be done and what actions are needed.

The case for improving the effectiveness of school interventions in cases of bullying is, I believe, overwhelming. But how is it to be done? I argue that, in the first instance, we need to recognize that far more attention needs to be paid to what can be done in addressing actual cases of bullying *as well as* seeking to create a school environment in which the task may be more manageable. Next, schools need to be aware of the range of approaches that may be adopted and applied in dealing with particular cases. The main purpose of this book is to promote an understanding of what methods exist and when and how they can best be applied.

Endnotes

1   The evidence on the effects of bullying on the health of children has been documented in numerous studies. For a summary of these effects, see Rigby (2003). It is known that children who have been psychologically damaged at an early age often continue to be affected in their adult years. In a recent Finnish study, young men were assessed for psychiatric symptoms when they registered for national service between the ages of

18 and 23 years. They had earlier, at the age of eight years, been assessed at school to discover whether they had been involved in bully/victim problems as bullies or victims. Those that had bullied others frequently or had been bullied frequently were approximately three times more likely than those who had not been involved in bullying at school to be classified as psychiatrically disordered (see Ronning *et al.* 2009).

2 Cross-national trends in bullying in schools in North America and Europe between 1994 and 2006 have been reported for the United States, Canada, and most European countries (Molcho *et al.* 2009).

3 These include evaluations of anti-bullying programs conducted by Smith *et al.* (2004c), Smith *et al.* (2004a); Vreeman and Carroll (2007); Baldry and Farrington (2007); Ferguson *et al.* (2007); Rigby and Slee (2008); and Mishna (2008). All agree in claiming that outcomes from interventions have been inconsistent and relatively little or no progress has been made in reducing bullying in schools. The most favorable of the evaluations as reported by Baldry and Farrington (2007) suggest that, in general, anti-bullying programs reduce victimization in schools by around 20 percent. By contrast, Ferguson *et al.* (2007) claim that school-based anti-bullying programs have proved to be 'ineffective in reducing bullying or violent behaviours in the schools' (p. 7).

4 How teachers can help children to become more resilient is set out in a helpful book by McGrath and Noble (2006).

5 'Circle time' involves students attending meetings conducted at intervals with a teacher who enables each of the participants in turn to explain and share what is on their minds, typically about school life, and to hear helpful suggestions from others in the group. It can help young people develop skills such as listening and empathizing and also build self-esteem and respect for others. On occasion, it can act as a forum at which the nature and effects of bullying can be considered and lead to the development of an anti-bullying code to which all members of the school community have contributed. See Mosley and Tew (1999) and Bellhouse (2009).

6 It has been claimed that bullying can be countered indirectly through the exercise of good classroom management (Roland & Galloway 2002).

7 Garrity *et al.* (1996) have provided extensive materials on how a school can be 'bully proofed.' Haber (2007) employs the same metaphor in claiming that a child can be comprehensively bully proofed – and for life!

8 An article published in the *Brown University Child and Adolescent Behavior* letter (2002) on behalf of the Menninger Institute is typical. It

claimed that a universal intervention to reduce bullying, targeting all students, was the most effective approach. Evidence was provided of increased empathy toward others and less supportive attitudes toward aggression, but, as in most other studies concerned with methods of preventing bullying through programs directed to all students, evidence of reduced bullying was notably lacking.

9 See Rigby (1996, 2008) on how parents and educators can reduce bullying in schools.

10 Based on an Australian sample of over 38 000 students, some 30 percent of respondents between the ages of 7 and 16 years reported that they had been bullied at school and had told a teacher about it (see Rigby 1997b). According to students, teacher interventions were successful in less than 50 percent of cases (Rigby & Barnes, 2002; Rigby, 2008).

11 The online survey was conducted by Rigby and Bauman in 2006. The results from the survey of US teachers and counselors were reported by Bauman *et al.* in 2008. Rigby and Bauman reported the results for Australian respondents in 2007. As details of teacher preferences for actions to address cases of bullying are highly relevant, they are given in full for US respondents in Appendix A.

Part 1

Interventions in Perspective

Before examining how best to intervene in cases of bullying, we need to place the subject of bullying in perspective. In Chapter 1, I consider how schools respond to bullying – and why their interventions are often ineffective. Especially important are the factors that make responding successfully to cases of bullying difficult and challenging. Tackling bullying is never easy.

Effective action is seen as first requiring a realistic grasp of what is known about the nature of bullying, the forms it takes, and its prevalence and harmfulness to the well-being of students of all ages. Chapter 2 provides a brief account of such essential knowledge.

Once this has been understood, the school can take steps to identify actual cases of bullying; that is, recurring patterns of aggressive behavior that are inflicting pain and suffering upon children who appear unable to defend themselves adequately – and who therefore need to be helped by the school. Chapter 3 discusses how sound judgments can be made about when interventions are required – leading on to the choice of the most appropriate way the school can act.

Bullying Interventions in Schools: Six Basic Approaches, First Edition. Ken Rigby.
© 2012 Ken Rigby. Published 2012 by Blackwell Publishing Ltd.

Chapter 1

The Current Situation

In the late twentieth and early twenty-first centuries, bullying in schools became a hot issue and a matter of public controversy. By that I mean a controversy held in public; not necessarily an issue discussed by the public. It was an issue taken up by the media – the newspapers, magazines, television, the innumerable producers of websites and, most distinctively, by radio commentators. And in this new controversy, there were almost always two strident protagonists.

Over there in the blue corner is the sentimental idealist dripping with empathy, full of the milk of human kindness. He or she knows full well what the bully is like. Beneath that belligerent exterior beats the heart of a sensitive and well-meaning person, driven to pathetic posturing by circumstances which the bully cannot control. The sentimental humanitarian knows well what needs to be done. The bully needs to be soothed. He must be treated with infinite kindness. At the root of his disorder is wounded self-esteem.

In the red corner, scarcely able to contain himself (or herself), is the emotional 'brutalitarian'.[1] He or she also knows full well what the bully is like. The bully is evil and must be crushed or otherwise

Bullying Interventions in Schools: Six Basic Approaches, First Edition. Ken Rigby.
© 2012 Ken Rigby. Published 2012 by Blackwell Publishing Ltd.

removed. The bully is the enemy; likewise, the hordes of hopeless do-gooders who infest Departments of Education and are thought to be doing nothing about the problem.

We meet these vivid characters when we open a newspaper or listen to talk-back radio. Naturally, it is the brutalitarian who takes the offensive. The sentimental humanitarian is, by and large, a straw man or a straw Department of Education.

Now the interesting thing is that these protagonists, real or imaginary, do their stuff on the public stage only, rather like Punch and Judy in the old days. The vast body of people see things differently. They recognize that each and every one of us is from time to time a bully – and a victim too. They also recognize that there are those in our community who really are a constant and serious menace, and that bullying constitutes a very serious problem indeed. The lives of innocent people are being damaged, in some cases irretrievably. Something must be done about it. But they see it as it is: not simplistically as the sentimental humanitarian and the emotional brutalitarian see it, but as a complex problem to which simplistic answers are absurd. The vast majority of the people see it as the American journalist H. L. Mencken perceptively observed:

> For every complex problem there is an answer that is clear, simple and wrong.[2]

This book is about what schools can do about this problem – by intervening in cases of bullying that come to their attention. It does not prescribe one method to fit all cases. Rather it seeks to describe what can be done, the reasons for adopting particular forms of intervention, and the evidence (where available) for believing that interventions in cases of bullying can be successful.

Again I must insist that the fact that this book is about interventions in cases of actual bullying should not detract from the highly important work that is being done in schools to prevent bullying from occurring in the first place, so that intervention becomes unnecessary. Like most other writers in this area, I fully commend the 'whole school approach' to bullying. This approach includes the development of an agreed school anti-bullying policy that ensures that pro-social behavior is encouraged, especially by working with children in classrooms to promote desirable values and the formation of positive and supportive relationships among children. But efforts at prevention directed toward the total school population without sufficient attention being paid to those who are most directly involved in the problem are not likely to achieve much success. For instance, curriculum-based social education delivered to all children, however desirable, has thus far produced disappointing results. In one recent meta-evaluation of published reports on work in classrooms to promote more pro-social behavior, it was found that, in most instances, there was no significant reduction in actual bullying.[3]

Much more work is needed. Especially, schools need to know what options are available when bullying actually takes place, as inevitably it will. Schools need to evaluate each one of the methods, appraising both its strengths and weaknesses, and exercise the best judgment as to whether it is to be applied in particular cases of bullying.

Perhaps the first thing to be recognized is that successful interventions to stop, or even to reduce, bullying in schools are difficult to achieve. As we have seen, thus far interventions to reduce bullying in schools have been only modestly successful. Reports from students who have sought help from teachers to stop them from being bullied often convey disappointment.

Yet it is fair to say that nowadays most schools, and arguably all educational jurisdictions, are taking the matter of bullying very seriously. Almost daily, schools encounter cases of bullying and do their best to stop them from continuing. Why then are the results so disappointing?

Why is Bullying so Difficult to Stop?

The first answer sometimes given is based upon conjecture about the history of human evolution. Put simply, humans, as well as all other creatures, are seen as programmed to bully others – if they can do so. In short, those who can, bully; those who cannot are the hapless victims. Yet as it stands, this is surely an extreme and questionable extrapolation from Darwinian theory. It can also be pointed out that many species, including our own, have survived and indeed thrived because of an inbuilt predisposition among its members to cooperate and work together for the good of all.

Nevertheless, physically aggressive behavior is characteristic of most young children. According to some researchers, it is at its most frequent among children between 18 months and four years. Seemingly, behaving aggressively does not have to be learned.[4]

Fortunately, most humans gradually and over time learn how *not* to be aggressive and find more socially desirable ways of achieving their aims. But a minority do not. Arguably, this is because their drive to act aggressively is particularly strong and/or they are not sufficiently influenced, largely by adults, to behave otherwise. Whatever the explanation, it is estimated that around 5 percent of children are likely to continue to act very aggressively and eventually to act in dangerously violent ways.

As well as these physically aggressive children, many of whom bully others at school, there are others whose aggressiveness mainly takes the form of verbally harassing others. In fact, most of the bullying that occurs involves verbal abuse which may on occasion lead to physical confrontations. In addition, there are more indirect forms of bullying, such as excluding people unfairly and sending nasty e-mails or text messages. The rise of cyber bullying in recent years has added a new dimension to the nature of peer victimization.[5]

When all the different forms of bullying have been summated to produce a general measure of bullying, certain trends have become evident in children's behavior. It is possible to identify different clusters of individual children. There are those children – a large proportion – who rarely or never engage in bullying behavior throughout their school careers. Some others bully to a moderate degree and the extent to which they bully others remains relatively constant during their years at school. Then there are a few who engage in a good deal of bullying to begin with but fortunately desist over time. Finally, there are those who engage in a good deal of bullying to begin with and maintain or increase their bullying behavior.

These consist of about 10 percent of children – and they constitute a major problem for schools.[6]

It is these children who are responsible for a very high proportion of the bullying that occurs in schools. It is these children that constitute the greatest difficulty that confronts teachers. Understanding why these children bully and how they can be handled is a major challenge for all schools.

We need to ask how these 10 percent or so of children get that way. The first answer I shall give is a highly unpopular one, rarely mentioned in writings on bullying. The fact, long dismissed by many developmental psychologists, is that there is a strong genetic influence at work. With the rise and rise of genetic psychology, it has become evident that some children are much more strongly predisposed than others to fill the roles of bully and victim. A careful study of the bullying tendencies of pairs of identical and fraternal twins published in 1960 suggested that genetic influence on bullying behavior of children was strong. The paper was generally ignored. A much bigger and more impressive study in 2008 produced quite similar results and, given the current zeitgeist, is being attended to. It was concluded that some 61 percent of the variation between children in bullying behavior could be accounted for by genetic factors and a slightly higher proportion (73 percent) in variation between children in being bullied.[7] From this study, other factors were comparatively unimportant in accounting for variations in children's bullying behavior or in being victimized by their peers.

It should be understood that genetic factors never operate in a vacuum. They affect behavior only through interaction with what is contributed by the environment. Thus, an environment that helps to overcome a child's predisposition to act aggressively, even a child who is strongly predisposed to act that way, may prevent a child from ever engaging in bullying. On the other hand, a quite mild predisposition toward behaving aggressively may result in a child becoming very aggressive if that child is brought up in a family or in a neighborhood which in some way encourages or gives license to violent behavior.

Now it is true that some children who are highly aggressive do not necessarily bully others; that is, they do not continually seek to dominate and abuse people weaker than themselves. They discharge their aggression in other ways. On the other hand, all bullies are by definition aggressive. Being aggressive by nature increases the chances that a child will bully – if he or she can.

The prime concern in this book is with the subgroup of aggressive children who continually bully others. Besides being predisposed to act aggressively, there are other important influences that help to determine how they will use or abuse their power over others. A good deal is now known, for instance, about how parenting and family life contribute to the genesis of bullying.[8]

It is known that the early experience of insecure attachment to a caregiver can increase the likelihood that a child will subsequently become involved in bully/victim problems at school. Placing young children in inadequate childcare centers at too early an age and for long periods of time can result in a child manifesting antisocial behavior later at school. Children brought up in dysfunctional and uncaring families are less likely than others to form positive relations with others at school. Cold, authoritarian parenting is apt to frustrate children and motivate them to act aggressively toward their peers. Socially prejudiced parents can pass on to their children attitudes that incline them to bully those who do not conform to accepted social stereotypes. These typically include ethnic groups and homosexuals. Neglectful parents who fail to keep track of their children run the risk of them becoming delinquent and acting violently toward others. Enmeshed families that limit the opportunities of their children to mix with other children before they go to school increase the chances that their socially unskilled children will be victimized at school.

I have listed above some major factors that contribute to increasing the difficulties faced by teachers when they seek to intervene, but there is one source of difficulty that will always escape detailed analysis. This difficulty relates to those events which are essentially unpredictable. Prominent among these involve the friendships that children make. Often entirely unexpectedly, a child meets another child or group and a bond or association is formed. How that child behaves subsequently will depend to a large degree on the pressures exerted by the group and the resistance or otherwise offered to those pressures.

In relation to many of these factors discussed above, the school can have, at best, quite limited influence: none as far as genetic influence is concerned; generally little or none in the use of appropriate child care and child rearing; a little perhaps in molding community social attitudes in the neighborhood, but then only in the long run and indirectly through the effects it has on its students. So what a school can do in effectively addressing bullying must inevitably contend with a wide range of countervailing factors, not least of which are the essentially unpredictable nature of individual behavior and the chance associations that members of the school community make with one another. Interventions are never going to be easy.

Try we must. But I say first we need to know what educators are up against in trying to stop the bullying and appreciate why the going is likely to be tough. We need to understand well the social context in which bullying occurs and the forces that can make the task of addressing cases of bullying so difficult. Only then can we effectively appraise the methods that schools are being asked to consider as the means of stopping the bullying.

The Case for a much Greater Emphasis upon How to Intervene in Cases of Bullying in Schools

It will, I hope, at this stage be obvious that I believe that every effort should be made to prevent bullying from ever happening. This means starting early, for instance, in promoting better child care and more thoughtful parenting. It means bringing about changes in society so that there is less encouragement and support for aggressive behavior and an end to social prejudice that underpins so much social discrimination. It means educating children in schools about bullying and engendering mutual support and cooperation. All these things and more are needed. Having said this, I strongly believe that there is a serious imbalance of attention being given to different aspects of the problem, with relatively little attention being paid to direct methods of intervention in actual cases of bullying. Allow me to recap and sharpen the argument.

1. Actual cases of bullying are not being dealt with well. Only a minority of children being bullied go to teachers for help. Overall, teachers are unable to help more than half of them – and much less than half of the adolescent students who need help.
2. Most schools exhort students who are being bullied to tell. Most students do not. Given the reluctance many students have to inform and the low level of confidence that many students have about whether teachers can help, this is not surprising.
3. Meanwhile a good deal of attention is being directed in some schools toward promoting constructive and socially positive ways in which all children can relate to each other happily.[9] What is sometimes not recognized is that most children do that. They do not bully, or do so rarely; most students are not bullied, except quite occasionally. Programs to improve the general ethos of the school may help. But for the most part their impact on bullying is limited. They may be said to help to make nice kids nicer and ensure that some of them will behave in a helpful and supportive way toward children who are being bullied. This is very desirable, as it can mitigate the negative effects of bullying. But the behavior of the minority of children who continually engage in bullying or suffer from being bullied is, I believe, affected to a minor degree, if at all.
4. Crucially, as many researchers have pointed out, the vast majority of cases of bullying involve a small minority of students, as either bullies, victims or bully-victims (i.e., children who bully others and are bullied themselves), and the causes of the bullying often lie outside the reach of the school. It is, in my view, these children who merit our greatest attention when we address the problem of school bullying. The damage they do to others and the harm they may do to themselves is incalculable.
5. Finally, teachers and often counselors are largely uninformed about what can in fact be done to address actual cases of bullying – as opposed to spreading good will. And they will remain so until there is sustained action in examining the options and providing pre-service and in-service training to acquire the necessary judgment and skills.

The Choice of Six

Why six? Inevitably the choice of six methods of intervention is to some extent arbitrary and reflects the judgment of the author. But these six comprise, to the best of my knowledge, the major approaches being undertaken by some schools at the beginning of the twenty-first century. They may be listed as follows:

1. The traditional disciplinary approach
2. Strengthening the victim
3. Mediation
4. Restorative Justice
5. The Support Group Method
6. The Method of Shared Concern

Each one of these methods or approaches has its supporters and practitioners. Personally, I believe that a case can be made out for each one in some circumstances, sometimes in combination with other methods. The approaches are not all mutually exclusive.

Some readers may feel that there are other ways that should have been included or at least considered. Perhaps the most obvious is to leave things alone in the belief that the students sort it out themselves. There *are* occasions when one may hesitate to act, that is, when it is unclear whether it really is a case of bullying. But as a general rule, ignoring the matter is rightly dismissed as not an option. Very few teachers are now prepared to ignore cases of bullying,[10] considerably fewer than was the case 50 years ago.

There are teachers who believe that an intervention can reasonably involve identifying children who are particularly inclined to bully and sending them away from their school to be handled by 'experts' in a special school. This is understandable, especially when one reflects upon the harm some persistent and recalcitrant children can do in hurting or disturbing others at school. It is felt that 'normal' children need to be protected from 'the likes of these'. Moreover, seemingly incorrigible children do need special attention and may be helped in centers where there are staff trained in behavior management. As a general rule, this approach is one that should only be considered in extreme cases. Wherever possible, cases of bullying are best addressed in the normal school environment.

For the moment I will stick with these six – until someone convinces me that there is yet another way.

Summary

This book addresses the problem of what schools can do when cases of bullying arise. It does so in the full recognition that there are no simple or obvious answers along the lines being promoted by the sentimental humanitarian or by the emotional brutalitarian, as so often portrayed in the media. It acknowledges that interventions to address school bullying have been largely unsuccessful, especially in secondary schools. It recognizes the great difficulties facing schools in attempting to eliminate bullying. To help teachers, it offers a description and a critical examination of the alternative forms of interventions that schools can use, in the hope that this will stimulate thought and provide some guidance for schools that are open to both new and old ideas about what can be done.

Endnotes

1   The term 'brutalitarian' was coined by G. K. Chesterton (1915) to describe the fanatical supporter of violent punishment as the appropriate treatment of criminals.

2   H. L. Mencken (1880–1956), was an American journalist, essayist, satirist and critic of American life, known as the Sage of Baltimore. The quotation attributed to Mencken, but not sourced, was found at http://quotationsbook.com/quote/32496/ (December 9, 2009).

3 In 10 studies that had evaluated the impact of a curriculum designed to reduce bullying, Vreeman and Carrol (2007) found that only four of them reported decreased bullying. Of these four, three of them showed no improvements in some populations in which they had been applied.

4 Canadian psychologists Richard Tremblay *et al.* (2004) have argued that aggressive behavior comes naturally to humans and is especially manifest in young children before they have learned to behave nonaggressively. Although approximately 28 percent of young children (between one and a half years and four) have been reported as showing little or no aggression, most infants do behave aggressively from time to time, with 14 percent classifiable as highly aggressive.

5 For a comprehensive overview of cyber bullying, see Kowalski *et al.* (2007) and Shariff (2008).

6 Pepler *et al.* (2008) have identified a subgroup of students (around 10 percent) who between the ages of 10 and 16 years frequently bully others and may become more aggressive as they grow older.

7 Because there was little acceptance until recently among developmental psychologists that genetic factors could strongly influence behavior, the research of O'Connor *et al.* (1980) was generally disregarded. More recently the influence of genetic factors has become widely recognized and the paper by Ball *et al.* (2008) has shown that involvement in bully/ victim problems at school has a strong genetic basis.

8 An account of the research linking parenting factors to subsequent and concurrent involvement of children in bullying in schools, as victims or as bullies, is provided in Rigby (1996) and more recently in a book written primarily to help parents (Rigby, 2008).

9 Perhaps the most comprehensive and well-documented attempt to reduce bullying largely through promoting social and emotional well-being among students is the *Friendly Schools and Families* Program (Erceg & Cross, 2004).

10 In the online survey reported by Rigby and Bauman (2007) and Bauman *et al.* (2008), less than 3 percent of teachers and counselors reported that they would ignore cases of low-level bullying. Almost certainly 15 years ago, the percentage would have been considerably higher.

Chapter 2

A Brief Background to School Bullying

It is generally agreed that intervening successfully in cases of bullying in schools is not easy. Interventions based upon the idea that bullying can be brought to an end by the teacher getting into a rage and dressing down the bully, or alternatively casually imposing a sanction such as a detention, are almost always quite futile. Telling the unrepentant 'bully' that, despite appearances to the contrary he or she is really a fine person, and as good as anyone else, is likely to prove equally futile. As we have seen, the reasons why a child engages in bullying may be complex and sometimes unclear. We need to be as well informed about bullying as possible before we begin.

The Concept of Bullying

We are inclined to think that the concept of bullying is one that requires little thought. It is commonly seen as evident. But for some it is not. It is, for example, often confused with aggression and with violence.

Bullying Interventions in Schools: Six Basic Approaches, First Edition. Ken Rigby.
© 2012 Ken Rigby. Published 2012 by Blackwell Publishing Ltd.

Bullying is aggression, but aggression as it occurs under particular circumstances. It can only occur when there is an imbalance of power between people; that is, when the person or persons acting aggressively are more powerful than the person or persons they are targeting. And of course the inequality in power may take many different forms. The aggressor(s) may be physically stronger, verbally more adept at hurting the other person, more socially skilled, or have a more imposing social status and/or more supporters. Bullying is not necessarily violent – unless the meaning of the term 'violent' is expanded, as it sometimes is, to include any hurtful act, including – some might say – an unkind word. As the word 'violent' is commonly understood, most bullying is not violent. Only a small proportion is, for example, aggression involving severe physical assault.

There is another consideration which is often ignored. This is whether the act of aggression was justified. To some, this consideration is irrelevant, as it is assumed that all acts of aggression are unjustified. No one, they say, should be attacked, no matter what they do. But rarely in practice do people take this stand. The policeman may overpower the robber; the soldier may fire on the enemy; the teacher may exclude the unruly student from the classroom; the student may strike back at his tormentor – in these and many other cases there may be justification or at least partial justification for a show of aggression. Hence, we must insist that bullying is always *unjustified* aggression. We must also recognize the fact that what is or is not justified is to some degree culturally determined – and that even within a particular culture individuals may make different judgments.

Finally, 'bullying' is commonly seen as part of a chain of events, occurring when an unjustified act of aggression against a less powerful target is repeated. Although the notion that bullying involves 'repeated behavior' is a widely accepted part of a definition of bullying, it is not without its dangers. It can result in a child's need for support being dismissed if he or she has been unfairly treated and even seriously hurt on only one occasion, even when those present have reasonably viewed it as bullying. It is sensible to allow for this possibility in defining bullying and say that bullying *typically* involves repeated acts of aggression. It is worth adding that it is currently controversial as to whether the concept of bullying must include reference to its repeated nature. Authorities in this area take up different positions.[1]

Identifying an act as bullying requires a series of steps which include:

- Identifying an act – or more commonly a series of acts – of aggression that are reliably observed or reported
- Judging that it is being perpetrated by an individual or group against whom the target is unable to offer adequate resistance
- Concluding that there is no justification for the attacks

The Prevalence of Bullying

Estimates of the prevalence of bullying vary enormously, depending upon how it is assessed. If you ask children whether they have ever felt they have been treated badly by another child, the prevalence rate can approach 100 percent. If you limit the instances to those involving grievous bodily harm, the rate drops to less than 5 percent. Between these extremes, a reasonable estimate can be obtained from anonymous responses to questionnaires, that is, if it is made clear that bullying occurs when the negative treatment has been perpetrated repeatedly by a more powerful person or group. Commonly such questionnaires allow the respondent to say how often the bullying has occurred over a given period of time. When this procedure is followed, typically about 50 percent respond by saying they have not been bullied. Around 15 percent say that they experience some form of bullying on a weekly basis. Of these some say they are not bothered by it. Children who are bullied most days and are likely to be seriously and perhaps permanently affected comprise around 5 percent.[2]

Teachers and parents sometimes see bullying as predominantly physical. In fact, verbal bullying is far more common, and often at least as hurtful. Indirect bullying such as exclusion, rumor spreading, and offensive electronic messaging can sometimes be the most hurtful of all and is about as common as physical bullying.

The Distribution of Bullying

Bullying behavior tends to become less common with age. There is one notable exception to this rule. In the early years of secondary school, it is generally higher than in the last year of primary school. This is true whether the transition is in Year 7 or in Year 8.[3] This suggests that changes in rates of bullying are at least in part determined by social factors, especially the coming together of children who do not know each other and who struggle to achieve dominance.

The nature of the bullying also tends to change according to age. Older children are less likely to engage in physical bullying and more likely to use verbal or indirect means, for example, excluding people or using electronic means of communication such as text messages. Finally, boys are more likely to engage in bullying than girls, at least in physical bullying. In other areas of bullying the differences tend to be small and not significant. Although cases of bullying can occur at any age and with either gender, they are most likely to involve boys and to occur especially in the early years of secondary school.

Developmental trends for subgroups of students

Although most children appear to bully less and to be bullied less often as they grow older, there are subgroups of children for whom this generalization does not apply. As noted earlier, there are some children who are never involved in bully/victim problems; there are some who desist from bullying as they grow older; and there are some who continue to bully others quite frequently, and may actually increase their bullying behavior. One cannot assume that a child will in time 'grow out' of bullying others. For some children, unless action is taken to change their trajectory of increasing aggression, things will probably go from bad to worse.

The Harm of Bullying

A remarkable change has occurred in society regarding the perception of the harm that bullying can do. It is now recognized that being subjected to continual and/or severe bullying can have very serious psychological consequences for the target. A large amount of research has accumulated, demonstrating that the stress induced by being victimized at school can lead to severe depression, suicidal thinking, and in some cases actual suicide.[4] Moreover the effects can be long lasting and result in adults who were bullied at school having low levels of confidence and bouts of anxiety. Children who constantly bully others at school often behave in an antisocial or delinquent way outside school, and unless they are helped to overcome their aggressive ways become a major threat to the wider community when they leave school.[5]

The relative severity of cases of bullying

Rating the severity of cases of bullying is important but difficult. In part, this is due to the fact that both subjective and objective considerations apply. If we infer degree of severity from the way the victim feels about what has happened, identical acts of bullying may give rise to different degrees of 'severity'. One child may be virtually unaffected by being taunted; another may be seriously upset. If we infer severity objectively from the intensity or frequency of the negative treatment as judged by an outsider or by how the *average* targeted person feels about it, we may fail to see how a given student is being affected by a particular insult. In general, sympathy for the victim may incline us to judge severity according to subjective criteria.

On the other hand, we may want to take into account the nature of the act as distinct from its effects; for instance, whether it is violent as in frequent physical beatings, or relatively mild as in an occasional slight. This becomes important when the school is deciding what kind of 'consequence' should apply in dealing with the bully. Practitioners with a legalistic approach to dealing with cases will especially want 'to make the punishment fit the crime'.

There is no correct answer to how to judge degrees of severity of bullying. And yet if we are to make commonsense decisions about what to do about bullying, assessments of severity may have to be made. Despite the real difficulties in making assessments of the severity of cases, there are practical advantages in attempting to do so. Teachers may feel they must prioritize and deal first with what they

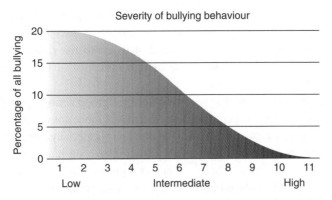

Figure 2.1 Continuum of bullying severity. From Rigby (2001, p. 31).

believe is most severe. They may also opt to use different intervention methods according to the severity of the bullying.

What I think we can say is that most cases of bullying are relatively mild; the extremely severe cases are much less common. It is useful to conceptualize bullying as lying along a continuum of severity, as in Figure 2.1.

Bear in mind that severity is not the same thing as culpability. Generally speaking, those who bully most severely are regarded as most culpable; but when bullying is provoked, as it is sometimes, the perpetrator may be judged as not really all that culpable. Nor is severity necessarily indexed by the harm that has befallen the victim. One would expect a close relationship between the severity of the bullying and the seriousness of the plight of the victim. However, one targeted person may be seriously hurt by bullying that seems mild to the observer; another may be so resilient as to be unharmed by bullying that seems very severe.

The Perpetrators

It is common to view the perpetrators as unusually aggressive and antisocial children – and indeed some are. But in many cases, the focus on individual characteristics or psychopathology is misguided. True, those who bully do tend to be generally more aggressive and less empathic than average, but there are numerous exceptions. Quite often, bullying behavior can be attributed less to the character of a particular individual than to the malign influence of the group to which that individual belongs.

Sometimes the bullying is carried out by a group acting in concert. Self-reports from students suggest that this is more common among girls than boys. Rather more students who bully (especially among boys) claim that they do so as individuals. Closer inspection however reveals that many children who bully are in fact supported and encouraged by their group of friends to target those whom their group dislikes.

A distinction should be made between perpetrators who are responding, at least initially, to a provocation, and those for whom there are no extenuating circumstances. These 'provoked' bullies are in a small minority. However, they do need to be identified when cases are being treated. A recent example in a South Australian primary school concerned a group of students of Italian background who were repeatedly harassing an Australian-born student who had been making racist comments about them. When intervening, a school may need to take into account the origins of the conflict. It is unwise to begin an intervention with a belief that the child who has engaged in bullying fits the usual stereotype.

The Targets

Distinctions should also be made between types of targets. Careful research on how victims of bullying behave toward others has revealed that about 15 percent of children who are repeatedly bullied actually bully other students.[6] Many of these may be described as 'provocative victims'. As noted earlier, some children actually provoke the bullying by behaving in ways that antagonize others. But for the most part children who are targeted are 'innocent', in the sense that they are not doing anything that can reasonably be called provocative.

It is sometimes apparent that a child is being targeted because of a social prejudice that exists in the community and/or among a group of students. The prejudice may relate to race or ethnicity, social class, disability, or sexual orientation. Alternatively, the bullying may be a response to a personal characteristic or idiosyncrasy that is perceived to warrant ridicule or even persecution.

A child may be targeted for any number of reasons – for looking 'different' from others in a conspicuous way, speaking differently, being 'smelly', having unusual interests, or even for having an odd name. Having an unusual personality may serve as a trigger: for instance, being highly introverted, depressed or timid, or, alternatively, being excessively 'loud' or insensitive to others. A social skills deficit may be at the root of the problem. Sometimes it is the way a child responds to being teased that leads to the bullying. Becoming enraged and seeming out of control can encourage the tormentors.

It is not always easy to identify the reasons for a child being bullied. For instance, a person who is a member of a minority ethnic group may or may not be a victim of prejudice. The bullying may derive from other sources, for instance, a perception that the child is personally obnoxious. The important thing is to keep an open mind on what the causes may be. In fact, one may never know. But one thing is clear. The longer the bullying continues, the more entrenched becomes the reputation of the target for being a 'victim' and the harder it is for the child to overcome the harm that is being done.

The Context of the Bullying

Naturally enough, the focus will be on the characters who are involved directly in the actual bullying: the bully or bullies and the target. It will be better at times to take a wider view of things. Especially, it can be very useful to know about the friendship group to which the perpetrator(s) belongs, and the bystanders who are commonly present when the bullying occurs.

Much has been said about the susceptibility of children to peer group pressure. The so-called peer group is generally a large group of young people who provide some normative pressure that influences students in the way they behave and interact with others. It can include all members of a class or even all members of a school. However, if we examine this large, somewhat amorphous group closely, we find that it is a complex body. Many of the students abominate bullying: some are indifferent, some are amused by it, and some find it attractive, even exhilarating. The proportions of those who exert a negative influence upon the social behavior of their peers, and those who are indifferent or positive, will vary from school to school and even from grade to grade. We know for instance that primary school students are generally much more empathic in their attitudes toward victims than children in early secondary school who, in turn, are less empathic than children in late secondary school.[7]

A much more intensive and influential pressure is provided by friendship groups. Some of these are very negative in their influence. They are sometimes referred to as gangs, but in many cases they are not conspicuous or violent in their behavior. Individuals who are part of such groups appear to share the same prejudices and may be fiercely intolerant of children who are targeted. Others follow 'the pack' because identifying with the group enables them to share in the 'success' or notoriety their behavior brings about; others follow because it is, in some circumstances, the safest course of action to take.

When bullying behavior actually takes place, those who are present may play a large part in how the action unfolds. When only the members of the friendship group are present, each of them can be expected to reinforce each other. They may act as a group or mob, or allow one or more of their group to engage overtly in the bullying, thus acting the part of an appreciative audience. Often, however, there are students present who are not part of the friendship group and these bystanders may at times speak up and discourage the bullying. Unfortunately they often do not do so.[8]

Summary

In preparing to intervene, an awareness of the main features of bullying is necessary. This includes an understanding of what constitutes bullying, the forms it may take, its prevalence, and the sad consequences that may flow from bullying having taken place. A common mistake is to fail to recognize the variety of types of individuals who become involved as perpetrators or targets of bullying in schools, and to implement interventions as if each case was basically the same. Of particular importance is the recognition that individuals may follow quite different trajectories in the nature of their interactions with their peers as they become older, with most children maintaining positive relations with their peers, some becoming notably less aggressive over time, and a small minority maintaining high levels of aggressiveness or becoming even more aggressive. It is this small minority of children that require the greatest attention and present the greatest challenges.

At the same time, all bullying occurs in a social context that strongly affects whether it continues. To understand how bullying develops and is supported or discouraged, it is necessary for schools to become aware of how bullying is influenced by the participants' friendship groups and the presence of bystanders when bullying takes place.

Endnotes

1   The leading authority on school bullying, Olweus (1993) asserted that bullying entailed "a pattern of behaviour repeated over time". The Anti-Bullying Alliance (ABA) in Britain maintains that bullying "is usually repetitive although some one-off attacks can have a continuing harmful effect on the victim". Concern is sometimes expressed over the possibility that occasionally cases of bullying may be dismissed on the grounds that an attack has happened on a single occasion.

2   These estimates are based on a large-scale Australian study (Rigby 2002b). But they are somewhat similar to estimates in other studies reported in Norway by Olweus (1993), in England by Smith *et al.* (2004), and in the United States by Seals and Young (2003). Minor variations in estimates are often due in part to variations in the wording of the questions that are asked of students and the response categories that are provided.

3   In some states of Australia such as New South Wales, children begin secondary school in Year 7; in some other states such as South Australia

they begin secondary school in Year 8. However, students in both of these states report an increase in bullying when they enter secondary school. The developmental stage appears to be less important than the effect of moving into a different sort of school environment. See Rigby (2002b) for details. Significant increases in reported bullying when children enter secondary school have also been reported by Pellegrini (2004) in the United States.

4 An examination of such effects may be found in Olweus (1993), Hawker and Boulton (2000), Bond *et al.* (2000), Rigby (1998, 2003, 2005a), and Rigby and Slee (1999).

5 The tendency for those who bully at school to act violently outside school and/or after leaving school has been documented by a number of researchers, including Farrington (1993) in England and Andershed *et al.* (2001) in Norway.

6 According to Solberg *et al.* (2007) approximately 10 percent of girls and 20 percent of boys who are continually victimized also bully others – and may well provoke others to bully them.

7 Generally children become less sympathetic toward victims of school bullying as they become older, that is, until they reach Years 10 and 11. At that stage, they typically become more supportive of those who are victimized by peers. See Rigby (1997a).

8 See Pepler and Craig (1995) for the seminal work on bystander behavior in primary schools.

Chapter 3

Preparing to Intervene

Incidents of bullying are exceedingly common. Every day, in every school, individuals are being subjected to unfair pressure by a more powerful person or group. Technically, they are being bullied. Life, as we soon learn as schoolchildren, is not fair. Does that mean that an intervention must be mounted every time someone is slighted or teased? Not at all. If every minor incident of bullying was investigated and addressed by school authorities, a great deal of the work of schools would come to a standstill. Incidents do not necessarily equate with cases.

When to Intervene

First, it must be confirmed that an act or a series of acts of aggression has actually taken place; that is, someone has deliberately sought to hurt or threaten another person. This is a necessary but not sufficient ground for identifying a case of bullying. As we have seen, aggressive behavior may not take the form of bullying, but it is always present when bullying occurs.

Bullying Interventions in Schools: Six Basic Approaches, First Edition. Ken Rigby.
© 2012 Ken Rigby. Published 2012 by Blackwell Publishing Ltd.

A difficulty sometimes arises when students are engaged in play-fighting, as is not unusual among boys and at times among girls. One can easily be deceived and jump to the wrong conclusion. Watch carefully. Are both parties having fun?

Denial by a victim of bullying that he or she is being bullied is not always conclusive. A targeted student may, on occasions, prefer a teacher not to intervene. The target may find the intervention deeply embarrassing or believe that it will be ineffective – or even likely to make matters worse. Despite strenuous denials by the victim the situation may need attention.

Whether help is given will depend in part on the wishes of the student. He or she may believe that the problem can be, or should be, solved without help. In cases where the harm being suffered appears to be great, the teacher may seek to persuade the student that help is needed and can be provided. Judgment will naturally be influenced by the student's parents, if they contact the teacher, and the opinions of colleagues.

Occasionally a teacher is confronted with what is, in a sense, the opposite situation. The student comes to the teacher claiming that he or she is being bullied when this is not so. The student is either over-sensitive or delusionary or possibly trying to get someone in trouble. This is rare, but the possibility should not be discounted. He or she may have been the object of not unreasonable criticism or subjected to (justifiable) exclusion. This does not mean that such a child should be dismissed. That child has a problem and may need counseling. But the problem does not entail bullying.

As previously explained, bullying can only occur in situations in which there is an imbalance of power between the aggressor and the target. However, the imbalance may sometimes be difficult to detect. The bullied child may be physically stronger than the tormentor, verbally more skilled, more popular – yet desperately miserable and unable or unwilling to provide an adequate defense. At the same time, the child may be suppressing as far as possible any signs of distress so as to avoid revealing any embarrassing weakness. Such a child may need the teacher's help.

One can sometimes be too ready to identify as a case of bullying a conflict in which two people are engaged in a heated argument or quarrel and one is getting the worst of it. Harsh words may be said and the two may come to blows. One of them may eventually break off, feeling defeated. In a sense, an imbalance of power has been demonstrated. But this is not necessarily bullying. There has been a 'fair fight' and one of them has lost. One may reasonably counsel the combatants and suggest that they settle their differences in a more civilized way; but it is far from reasonable to identify the victor as the bully – unless he or she subsequently imposes unfairly and repeatedly on the other.

Perhaps the hardest decision one may have to make in identifying bullying occurs when the aggressor has been deliberately provoked by the person who is, as a consequence, being targeted. One may think it entirely understandable for the aggressor to have hit back verbally or even physically, especially when he or she has been insulted or injured in some way. But the aggressor's behavior must be seen as unreasonable if it persists after the initial reaction, or is disproportionate to the degree of provocation. The fact that a targeted student has behaved provocatively in no way justifies any bullying behavior that it may elicit. Because both parties may be seen to be 'at fault' does not excuse inaction on the part of the teacher. But it does present a problem in dealing with the situation, as we shall later discover.

What is an Intervention?

The term 'intervention' is often loosely used. Sometimes it is assumed that if an anti-bullying policy is operating (and most, if not all schools in most countries claim that they have such a policy), then the school is 'intervening'. This is not the sense in which I am using the term. In this book I am concerned with 'case intervention' and have in mind *an act or series of acts designed to deal with a case of bullying behavior and to prevent its continuation.* The intervention may be conducted by a single practitioner – usually a counselor or teacher – or a team of practitioners or (on occasion) a student or students.

A further distinction can usefully be made between

1. What is done when bullying behavior is witnessed and immediate action is taken on the spot to deal with the situation, and
2. What is done to address specific cases of bullying according to a method of intervention that is designed to resolve the problem.

In this book I will be dealing principally with the second point, that is, methods of intervention that are designed to resolve the problem, taking into account what is seen as relevant about the case from available sources. But a few words about the first point are in order, that is, what may be done when bullying behavior is directly witnessed.

Intervention on the spot

If a teacher happens to witness bullying during a lesson break, it is likely to stop when the teacher appears. But it may not. The perpetrator may feel that his or her behavior is unexceptional, especially if it consists of teasing or can be construed as 'rough and tumble'. The target may collude with the perpetrator, not wanting the teacher or bystanders to get the impression that he or she is the sort of person who complains about such treatment. (It may still be desirable to consider how the target may come to see that it is in his or her best interest to receive help.) The teacher may sometimes decide to try to resolve the problem then and there. When the bullying is mild and the children involved are amenable, the teacher may indeed be able to take appropriate action, for example, by pointing out the unacceptability of the behavior and/or the harm the bullying may be doing to the target. However, in many cases, dealing effectively with the incident on the spot can be difficult, especially if the participants in the bullying are highly emotional and when bystanders are likely to play a negative role in the proceedings, and it is often sensible to arrange for the participants to meet with the teacher or counselor some time later, when the problem (which may be ongoing) can be addressed more objectively.

Two other situations may arise when the bullying is witnessed. The bullying may be observed taking place in the classroom and creating a disturbance. In this case, it may be sensible to ask the children involved in the incident to leave the class and receive help from a counselor or welfare person. Finally, in a few cases, the bullying may continue despite the teacher demanding that it should stop. In such circumstances, the teacher must make a note of who is involved and arrange for them to be seen later. Where the bullying involves physical violence, it may be necessary for the teacher to call upon the help of colleagues or even the police.

Intervention by bystanders

Bullying typically takes place with bystanders present and bystanders can play an important part by intervening. However, interventions by bystanders are relatively rare. For the most part bystanders merely stand and watch.[1] Efforts by teachers to promote effective bystander behavior can result in some bullying behavior being discouraged – at least temporarily.[2] Generally speaking, cases of bullying are unlikely to be *solved* by bystanders expressing their disapproval of the bullying behavior, though their contribution can be significant.

Sources of Information About Bullying Behavior

Although information about bullying obtained by staff members who witness incidents is particularly valuable, it is generally quite limited. In part, this is because bullying behavior tends to be hidden from teachers. They are not there where most of the bullying takes place – in the school grounds, on the way to school, on the way home from school, and on transport to and from the school. True, some bullying occurs in the classroom but it is mostly covert and not so conspicuous. A teacher engrossed in the task of teaching may not notice it. However, there are a number of other ways in which a case of bullying may come to the attention of the school without a staff member witnessing it.

The targeted child may come to a teacher or counselor to obtain help from being bullied. This is much more likely to occur among young children than among adolescents. In part, this is because younger children believe (correctly) that teachers are more able to help to stop the bullying.[3]

For the older student, there is more shame or stigma attached to telling a teacher. Moreover, there is always the danger that the perpetrators will find out that the target has 'told' and become motivated to make matters worse. Not surprisingly, many children endure being bullied rather than inform a teacher.[4] They are in fact more likely to tell a friend or tell a parent. Hence, this important source of information about bullying is often denied to the school. It cannot be overcome by simply exhorting children to make ours into a 'telling school'. But it can be changed by the school demonstrating that it is safe to tell and that interventions can succeed.

Teachers sometimes worry that some children will tell them that they are being bullied in order to get someone into trouble or even to draw attention to themselves. This is rare. It is much more likely that an informant has thought of telling a teacher on many occasions but had doubts about the wisdom of doing so, until in desperation the child has decided to tell. This does not mean that the informant has played no part in provoking the bullying or in exacerbating it. This may or may not come to light eventually. But certainly the accounts of children who come to a teacher to seek help must be taken very seriously.

Information about a case of bullying is often sought from a suspected target after there have been reports from other sources, such as other students. Such a child may, on occasions, deny that bullying has occurred or assert that he or she can handle it without the help of teachers. Normally, however, the child is grateful for support, especially if credible assurances are given that any disclosures will be handled confidentially and that there are grounds for believing that the situation can be improved.

The parents of the target constitute another source of information about the bullying. Understandably, their accounts of what has happened may be highly emotional and not always accurate. They are generally reliant upon what they have been told by their children and the events they describe may be misunderstood or distorted. Their accounts need to be corroborated. At the same time, they can provide unique information about how a target has been affected by treatment from peers. One should be more skeptical of accounts given by parents of the suspected bully when they are interviewed. A natural tendency is for parents to defend their child's behavior, however culpable it may seem. Yet there may be something in what they say. Their child may have been provoked.

Children who have witnessed what has been taking place can provide useful information. They are more likely to understand what is going on than adults. However, they may have different perspectives or motives in describing what they have seen. These bystanders may be performing different roles. It is known that some are assistants or supporters of those actually seen to be doing the bullying. Others may be defenders of the target. Yet others may be detached observers. It can be important to determine what role a bystander is performing when appraising the objectivity of an account.

Finally, in some schools there are more formal or mechanical ways of obtaining relevant information about who is involved in bullying incidents. One is the use of the bully audit, a device that enables students to provide written information identifying those who are being bullied or engaging in bullying others. This may be conducted using a 'bully box' into which students slip written statements about who is bullying someone. In some schools, students are advised to provide such information to a nominated staff member. Alternatively, the students in a class may be asked to nominate those who fit the categories of bully or target. Generally the informer is allowed to remain anonymous. This approach is controversial. Some teachers believe that it can lead to the school identifying students who would not otherwise be identified as bullies or victims. They may also argue that the procedure can empower students to bring about action that can help to establish better peer relations. On the other hand, some teachers oppose the use of a bully audit because they fear that some individuals will be accused falsely by their peers and that, in any case, students should not be encouraged to make negative judgments about others. A further method of identifying those involved in bullying is the use of video cameras strategically placed as a means of surveillance. In extreme circumstances this may be justified, for example, to identify cases of physical violence. At the same time, it is worth remembering that a great deal of bullying is not of a physically overt nature and cannot be captured in visual images.

Purposes of gathering the information

The more sources of reliable and corroborating information available about what has been happening between students who may be involved in a bully/victim problem, the greater will be the certitude that an intervention is either justified or not justified. This is why such 'background work' is so obviously useful. But there is another reason that is sometimes given for collecting such information. It is to provide evidence that can be used to 'try' the bullies and reach a just verdict, leading to the imposition of an appropriate consequence. For some teachers this is almost self-evident. For others it is highly debatable. For them, the gathering of information is important as a means of bringing about a resolution of the conflict, not necessarily in providing a 'just' outcome. As we shall see, the differences between those who focus upon 'justice' and those who focus upon a solution to the problem are not always easy to reconcile.

Summary

Interventions to stop bullying include (i) steps that need to be taken when incidents of bullying are directly witnessed and (ii) procedures that may be followed when it is decided that a case of bullying needs to be investigated and solved. This book is primarily concerned with the latter: interventions after cases of bullying have been identified. Relevant information to decide what action (if any) is needed may sometimes be gathered through direct observation by teachers in the playground and in classrooms, but is more likely to be obtained less directly from one or more sources. These include the targeted child, parents, bystanders, 'bully audits', and through video surveillance. Care is needed in evaluating the validity of information received from each of these sources. The purpose to which such information may be put will depend in part on the aim of the intervener, especially whether it is to achieve 'justice' for the target or to establish better relations between those involved in the problem. These aims may sometimes be in conflict. The approach or method chosen in particular cases may reflect the prime purpose of the intervention.

Endnotes

1   In Canada, Pepler and her coworkers (see Pepler & Craig 1995) estimated that on approximately 85 percent of occasions when school bullying at primary school occurred, bystanders were present, but on less than 20 percent of the time were attempts made by bystanders to stop it.

2   Menesini *et al.* (2003) in Italy has demonstrated that bystanders can be influenced by teachers to intervene. According to Rigby and Johnson (2006), this is more likely to occur when peer group pressure is mobilized to bring this about.

3   In a study of Australian secondary school students by Rigby and Bagshaw (2003), it was reported that most students, especially older students, believed that teachers were unable to help them if they were being bullied at school.

4   The dilemmas facing students when they consider whether they should tell a teacher are examined in detail in Rigby and Barnes (2002).

Part 2

Methods of Intervention in Cases of Bullying

Part 2 is about actual methods of intervention. Each of the next six chapters is devoted to a particular method of intervention in cases of bullying that can be used by a practitioner who is conversant with the method or, in some cases, trained in its application.

In the main, the interventions involve staff members rather than students as practitioners. Although peers in a school are sometimes trained to fulfill roles that may contribute to the resolution of bully/victim problems, their role tends to be secondary or limited in some ways. For instance, student members of a 'bully court' may assist staff in reaching a decision regarding the culpability of an offender and recommend that he or she should receive a sanction or penalty. But the school staff are ultimately responsible for the steps that are taken. Peer counselors may be trained and given the authority to counsel students who have become involved in bully/victim problems, essentially by listening and considering ways in which the problem may be solved. In doing so, they may play a useful role – especially since many students are more ready to seek help from their peers than from teachers. But their role is limited to applying

Bullying Interventions in Schools: Six Basic Approaches, First Edition. Ken Rigby.
© 2012 Ken Rigby. Published 2012 by Blackwell Publishing Ltd.

skills of mediation and support, typically in cases of relatively low-level bullying or harassment.

The intervention methods described in this book are ones undertaken primarily by school staff, in some cases with the valuable assistance of students and parents. Each is described in turn, together with its rationale. There follows a critique of the approach, examining both strengths and limitations. Where possible, the available evidence regarding its effectiveness is provided. Suggestions are made about situations or circumstances in which each method can usefully be employed.

Chapter 4

The Traditional Disciplinary Approach

The traditional way of dealing with school bullying, as with other kinds of antisocial or delinquent behavior, has been to discipline the offenders. In western countries, justification for this approach is often traced to writings in the Old Testament, where it is suggested that if you 'spare the rod' you will 'spoil the child'.[1]

Disciplined behavior in children, so it is often said, requires that sanctions – not necessarily physical ones – must be applied if the more powerful child is not to take advantage of a capacity to impose upon the weaker child. Combine this injunction with another Old Testament saying, "an eye for an eye and a tooth for a tooth",[2] and the appeal to many who are responsible for controlling the moral behavior of young people is irresistible. Not surprisingly, it has been estimated that approximately 75 percent of teachers believe that even relatively mild cases of bullying should be dealt with by punishing the perpetrator.[3]

For some writers there appears to be no other method worth considering. Statements such as the following occur with remarkable regularity in books and articles on bullying:

Bullying Interventions in Schools: Six Basic Approaches, First Edition. Ken Rigby.
© 2012 Ken Rigby. Published 2012 by Blackwell Publishing Ltd.

> Send a clear message that bullying will not be tolerated in your school
> and that all bullying incidents will be disciplined consistently according
> to procedures developed by the staff.[4]

And here from an Internet 'expert' on bullying:

> Any child who willingly bullies another should be set upon by someone
> stronger than he or she … and made to endure what he or she caused
> to her victims. 3 times over.[5]

Although the traditional disciplinary approach has been accused of
encouraging vindictiveness on the part of authorities, its proponents
are generally less concerned with obtaining 'revenge' or 'justice' than
in getting children to behave better: in short, to behave in a disciplined
manner. The notion of what makes up good or disciplined behavior
may differ from place to place and time to time. In Nazi Germany in
the 1930s and 1940s, it consisted of blind obedience to the commands
of the state, whatever they might be. But it would be unfair to characterize the application of this traditional approach to school bullying as
essentially due to the presumed authoritarianism of schools. It would
be more reasonable to see it as a means by which schools believe they
can achieve several desired goals. These may be summarized as follows:

- To discourage bullying behavior among offending students so that
  they cease to bully and begin to act in a more positive and
  disciplined manner
- To deter others from bullying by making them aware of the
  consequences that will be applied if they engage in bullying others
- To make it safer for children who might otherwise be bullied
- To deal justly with the offenders – the 'bullies' – by imposing an
  appropriate punishment

Essentially, the cessation of bullying is seen as being achieved through
the school making demands upon the perpetrator(s), backed up by
measures designed to produce compliance. These measures are typically punitive. But it should also be recognized that the personal
influence of the practitioner may also play a part. Children may begin to
behave in a 'disciplined way' under the influence of the school authority

for a variety of reasons, including fear, but also from a conviction that they should 'do as they are told' by a legitimate and rational authority. Hence, the traditional disciplinary approach may be exercised in a ruthless and authoritarian manner, or in a firm, authoritative way that respects the individual offender while insisting on compliance.

The Traditional Disciplinary Approach in Practice

There are some variations in the application of this method, but it generally involves these elements:

1. The determination of what constitutes bullying behavior.
2. The establishment of rules or guidelines that enable practitioners of the method to decide what actions are to be taken if the rules are broken.
3. Informing *all* members of the school community of what bullying is and what is to be done about it.
4. An investigation of cases of bullying to determine the culpability of the offenders. This may involve examining reports, talking to witnesses, and cross-examining suspected perpetrators.
5. The application of an appropriate sanction, penalty, or punishment. These may include 'time-out', detention, loss of privileges, chores that must be undertaken at the school, and, in more extreme cases, internal or external suspension.

There can be additional elements. For instance, the formation of the rules may be influenced by discussions with students in the classroom.[6] It seems reasonable to suppose that if students have a voice in suggesting what rules may best govern their relationships with each other, they will be more amenable to accepting them when they are applied. As well, in real-life cases, practitioners commonly do not apply the rules mechanically. They seek to explain or justify their actions, and sometimes engage in serious talks with children who have bullied and – in extreme cases – with their parents. Finally, the practitioner may sensibly decide to monitor the outcome and positively reinforce actions that are seen as helpful or pro-social and incompatible with engaging in bullying.

There is another application of the traditional disciplinary approach, one which places a good deal of responsibility on students themselves for any disciplinary action that may be taken – or more precisely on a group of nominated or elected students who make up a so-called bully court.[7] Such a group of students is empowered to 'try' suspected bullies, who are referred to them according to well-defined judicial procedures. They may question relevant persons in order to obtain an accurate picture of what has been happening to any students who may have been repeatedly victimized by a peer or peers. The court then deliberates and may recommend an appropriate sanction, with the understanding that the recommendation may or may not be accepted by the school authorities.

The bully court has two advantages over a disciplinary method which involves only members of the school staff. First, the students who comprise the 'court' may be able to form a better judgment of the behavior of those whom they examine. They are likely to understand their peers and their motives better than teachers can. It may be that the judgments of the fellow students are more acceptable than those made purely by the school staff – and therefore more binding. For many students, teachers constitute authority figures whom they do not trust. There is good evidence that the use of bully courts is, in fact, popular among students. On the other hand, there is an understandable fear among many teachers that the method could be abused by some groups of students who are 'out to get' those they dislike and that greater objectivity and fairness will eventuate when judgments are made by teachers acting *in loco parentis*. Not surprisingly, the use of 'bully courts' by schools is relatively rare.

Critique

The traditional disciplinary method is popular in most schools and this has the effect of facilitating its acceptance and consequent use by practitioners. Such popularity makes a 'whole school approach' to countering bullying more attainable. The school and the community can get behind it. This is important because an alternative approach that is less popular – and possibly more divisive – is unlikely to enjoy widespread support. It may therefore be less wholeheartedly implemented and, as a consequence, be less effective. Parents tend to be more supportive of a disciplinary approach – especially if their children are being bullied at school. This approach promises to involve the administration of justice. There is often a widespread fear in the community that offenders – for this is how those who bully are commonly seen – will 'get away with it' unless the school authorities 'come down hard upon them'.

The disciplinary approach is commonly viewed as straightforward: the rules of behavior established by the school are invoked, cases are investigated, and the transgressors duly punished. This apparent simplicity is contrasted with other more complex approaches in which counseling approaches are employed.

By stating the consequences in advance, the school can represent the outcome for the bullies as being brought about by their own actions. Sometimes the consequences are described as 'natural consequences'. This enables the school to avoid any charge that their own actions are in any sense arbitrary, vindictive, or vengeful. This way of looking at it is appealing to many schools.

Finally, there is a belief that by foreshadowing or applying appropriate sanctions, children who engage in bullying will not *dare* to continue in their 'evil ways' and will desist forthwith. Seeing what can happen to those who bully will discourage those who might otherwise engage in bullying. Innocent children will be safer.

How far these views are tenable is a matter of some controversy. First, it may be argued that the popularity of a method is not good evidence for its effectiveness. It is recognized, for instance, that there is popular support for the death penalty, but its abolition has not led to an increase in homicide.

The presumed straightforward nature of the traditional disciplinary approach can be illusory. It is true that there are acts performed in the course of bullying that are readily definable and identifiable. A child repeatedly striking another child is such an example, although to be sure that it involves bullying one needs to know more, for instance, whether it occurs in a situation in which there is an imbalance of power and whether the act was unjustifiable. There are many other acts that may constitute bullying which are much less easily identified and more difficult to encapsulate in school rules. Negative verbal behavior may on occasions be a possible indicator of bullying; on other occasions it may be regarded as justifiable criticism. Most striking, however, is the difficulty of framing rules that include indirect bullying, such as excluding or avoiding individuals or spreading malicious gossip. It is no answer to say that such behavior is of relatively little importance. There is evidence that it is the most hurtful of all forms of bullying.[8]

Efforts to provide rules that are unambiguous and specific may sometimes produce very questionable and even absurd results. In one school I visited, words as used by children were identified by the school as having degrees of offensiveness. Sanctions were imposed proportionate to how objectionable the words were, as rated by the school. Some words were seen as deserving a 'red card'; some a 'yellow card' deserving a lesser penalty. The context and intention behind the use of the words was ignored. Another example from a different school was to outlaw all behavior that involved touching another person, regardless of the intention of the toucher. The rule in this case was to cover physical bullying, but it covered a great deal of acceptable behavior as well. This apparent obsession with physical forms of bullying may derive in part from a school's desire to produce rules that are manifestly operational. It can unfortunately lead to a school ignoring a great deal of everyday and highly harmful kinds of bullying.

A major claim made by the practitioners of the disciplinary method is that it is the most practical approach. This may be considered first in the light of existing theory about the deterrent effect of imposing sanctions or punishment to reduce undesired behavior and, secondly, to examine what evidence exists regarding its effectiveness.

The Limited Effectiveness of Punishment

A large body of knowledge has been amassed to determine how behavior is affected by punishment. Some of it derives from the work on classical conditioning pioneered by Pavlov.[9] Broadly, he held that when a strong physiological or emotional response was elicited by an 'unconditioned' stimulus – as for example when a punishment is imposed – the effect of that stimulus, say fear, is transferred to other stimuli present at the time, ones that are not normally associated with the unconditioned stimulus. Thus, the person administering the punishment becomes someone to be feared. The student who has been punished will not want to come before him or her again, and will subsequently be compliant and desist from bullying. In future, the appearance of the child whom the bully had targeted may also evoke feelings of anxiety in the bully. The very thought of bullying that person or, perhaps more generally, any other person, becomes painful. How this process might work out has been dramatized in the film, *A Clockwork Orange* in which an adolescent boy is 'cured' of his love of indiscriminate violence by being 'conditioned' in a laboratory, so as to find engaging in aggressive and delinquent behavior abhorrent and unthinkable.[10]

In practice, conditioning a child in this way to put a stop to bullying may require very powerful and almost certainly unethical forms of treatment. Seeking to change the behavior of those who bully through fear-inducing methods is unlikely to find serious support among many educators. Nevertheless, in *some children*, having been punished, even relatively mildly, for engaging in bullying may inhibit their expression of aggressive behavior.

In the 1960s, a somewhat different way of understanding how behavior can be influenced was proposed and promoted, principally by behaviorists led by the American psychologist, B. F. Skinner.[11] This became known as operant conditioning. It was suggested that behavior is controlled by the nature of the events that have occurred after the behavior has taken place. Put simply, a child does things for which he or she has been rewarded, and avoids or desists from doing things which have been followed by aversive events. Numerous experiments were performed, mainly with rats and pigeons, to show how specific behaviors could be strengthened by being positively reinforced and weakened by being negatively reinforced or punished. From these experiments, a number of generalizations were made and held to be applicable to human behavior. It was proposed that individuals act as they do *entirely* because of their unique history of reinforcement. Their behavior could change only after it had been reinforced differently.

Of particular relevance to the use of the disciplinary approach was the claim that when actions are followed by aversive consequences, such as a penalty or punishment, they will *under some circumstances* become less likely to recur. The circumstances appear to include the following:

- Punishment is delivered *shortly* after the act of bullying and becomes associated with that event.
- The punishment *invariably*, or *almost invariably*, follows the act of bullying. (Each time the bullying occurs without being detected and punished, the effect of the treatment weakens or extinguishes.)
- The probability of punishment following an act of bullying is perceived as high and bullying is considered not worth the risk.
- The discouraging effects induced by the punishment are more powerful than the positive reinforcement that could be achieved by engaging in the bullying. Bear in mind that positive reinforcement of bullying may include observing the submission of the targeted person (in itself reinforcing for some perpetrators), and also the perceived or actual approval of the bullying provided by friends and bystanders – such reinforcement can be very powerful.
- The intensity or severity of the punishment is sufficient to produce the intended effect.

These conditions listed above are often not easy to satisfy in the school situation. There may be, unavoidably, a relatively long interval between the act of bullying and its detection and punishment. The bullying may occur quite frequently without being detected, especially if it is covert and relatively unobtrusive. The bullying may not come to the school's attention because the targeted person is reluctant to inform for fear of recrimination. The person engaged in the bullying may come to believe that the likelihood of being detected is low. The punishment available to the practitioner may pale in significance compared with the pleasure enjoyed by the bully in dominating someone and being admired by others for doing so. To increase the likelihood of success, the practitioner must control or counter all the various factors that blunt the effectiveness of the disciplinary action.

A further consideration concerns the reaction of the bully to the way he or she is treated by the disciplinarian. If the child comes to believe that the punishment was unjust, it may arouse a strong degree of resentment and a desire to continue the bullying, often in ways that are difficult to detect. A sense of injustice on the part of the punished person is, on some occasions, difficult to avoid given that bullying is sometimes provoked by the target of the bullying, and determining the level of punishment that is appropriate can be difficult for the school to achieve. Yet, if the disciplinarian is going to be successful in helping the bully to see the 'folly of his ways', justice must be seen to be done.

Thus far this critique has relied largely on psychological theory and speculation. Unfortunately, directly relevant empirical studies of the effects of the traditional disciplinary approach in dealing with cases of bullying are notably sparse. Of the anti-bullying programs that make use of sanctions and punishments, perhaps the Olweus Bullying Prevention Program is the most relevant, although it is evident that the Olweus program also contains a number of other features designed to promote positive and constructive behavior.[12] Nevertheless, his approach does stress the importance of taking firm punitive action to deal with cases of bullying and that by doing so schools can 'send a message' to everyone that bullying is not to be tolerated. Reported outcomes from the application of this program have been extremely variable. It is claimed in several studies undertaken in Norway that its use has been followed by a reduction in peer victimization by as much as 50 percent. However, in reported applications outside Norway, for example, in Germany, Holland, and in North Carolina in the United States, significant reductions have rarely occurred.

One study may shed some light on the effects of applying negative consequences when school children break school rules. The use of 'reinforcement theory' was a feature of a relevant study reported from the United States. Middle school students (Years 6, 7, and 9) in Oregon were taught school rules relating to appropriate social behaviors. Mildly negative consequences were applied when students were observed violating those rules, for example, by bullying others. They were also commended and reinforced when they were observed behaving in a notably pro-social way. In a careful evaluation of the effects, there were no significant changes in the reporting of physical or verbal aggression at school.[13] In this case, the intervention to reduce aggressive behavior was unsuccessful, despite the additional use of positive reinforcement on occasions when desirable behavior was observed. More studies of this kind are needed to evaluate the effects of the disciplinary approach.

One criticism of the traditional approach is that it is seriously misguided over what is needed to bring about 'disciplined behavior'. The assumption is that when children are deterred from acting anti-socially, they will be open to engaging in pro-social behavior, especially if they are rewarded or praised afterward for doing so. Quite apart from the question of whether practitioners can successfully reduce bullying using this method, there is the question whether *truly disciplined behavior* is producible by simply reinforcing the behavior required by the school. Some argue that disciplined behavior involves an unforced commitment to act in accordance with one's core values; that is, a process of internalization must occur rather than mere compliance.[14] In the case of children who repeatedly bully and enjoy the effects they are producing in those they victimize, this involves a real 'change of heart'. The question is: Can such a change be brought about through an essentially punitive approach?

Certainly the history of penology demonstrates that punishments, especially when they are extreme, have limited deterrent effect and tend to increase resentment and hostility toward those who inflict them. As one leading psychiatrist has observed: "The people whom we most wish to punish are the least likely to respond to punishment."[15]

A further criticism of this approach is that in focusing on the culpability of offenders, it fails to recognize that bullying is often a group phenomenon, and responsibility for its occurrence is diffused among the group members.

The Future of the Disciplinary Approach

Given that some form of punishment for the offense of bullying is widely supported in schools and in the community, it is highly likely that this approach will continue to be the primary way in which interventions are conducted for some time. Whether it is used less often as time goes by will depend in part on whether it can resist or refute the criticisms that are increasingly being raised against its application or its overuse.

It seems likely that, as alternative methods of intervention are increasingly considered, schools will be more discriminating in their selection of cases for which a traditional disciplinary approach is appropriate. Almost certainly a punitive approach will continue to be applied in cases of bullying that are very severe and can reasonably be described as criminal, such as continual and premeditated assaults. Community pressure will probably ensure that in such cases the law will apply and punitive actions will be taken; in some instances, legally sanctioned community conferences may be held to seek a resolution of the problem through the use of Restorative Justice.[16] But in a large number of cases, bullying does not involve criminal behavior, and other alternative and more effective treatments will, I believe, be increasingly considered by schools.

The age of the children involved in the bullying may influence the choice of method. There is some evidence that the Olweus anti-bullying program which emphasizes the use of disciplinary action in dealing with bullying is more successful with younger children than older secondary school students.[17] One possible explanation for this is that the behavior of younger children is more easily controlled by the use of punishment, whereas older children are more likely to resist what they see as authoritarian coercion. They are also more likely to believe that they can continue to bully without being found out. With young children, relatively mild forms of punishment – such as 'time-out' – may be sufficient to deter them from continuing to bully, as well as providing them with an opportunity to 'cool off'. It remains true, however, that very serious forms of bullying of a criminal nature are more likely to be perpetrated by adolescents and legally require a punitive response.

I believe that it will be some time – if ever – before the traditional disciplinary approach in dealing with bullying is abandoned. It may be helpful therefore to close this chapter with suggestions as to how the approach can be used more effectively and with more justification.

- Make it as clear as possible to the staff and to students what bullying is, the forms it takes, and especially the harm it does.
- Carry out classroom discussions with students on the issue of bullying and especially on the kinds of rules that ought to govern relations between students in the school. Have the class compile a list of reasonable guidelines for student behavior.
- As far as possible, gain acceptance from the student body that some 'consequences' are justified in cases of bullying. When more students are involved in the formulation and development of anti-bullying policy, acceptance will be more widespread.
- Intervene *as soon as possible* after an act of bullying has been identified so that the memory of the nature of the offense is present in the bully's mind.
- Where possible, apply punishments that are appropriate to the misbehavior, for example, ones requiring recompense and restorative action to be undertaken rather than largely unrelated impositions such as writing 'lines'.
- Apply positive reinforcement whenever the child acts constructively or helpfully toward another child, thus setting up habits that are incompatible with bullying.
- Engage in 'serious' talks with the person to be punished (and if appropriate the parents too), giving the reasons for the actions being taken by the school.

- Maintain a practice of rigorous surveillance of children's interpersonal behavior in the classroom and playground. Punishment is more likely to work if behavior is being carefully monitored.
- Do whatever is possible to ensure that the authority of the school and teachers is justified and respected. This is particularly important among older students who are generally more distrustful of institutional authority than younger students.
- Recognize that any action taken by teachers at the school that is widely seen as unfair or arbitrary will increase the distrust and disrespect felt by students, and result in disciplinary action taken in cases of bullying being much less effective.

The above suggestions, remember, are ways in which the use of disciplinary methods can be made more justifiable and effective. They do not necessarily endorse its use. Before committing to this approach, I strongly recommend a close examination of the other approaches given in subsequent chapters, especially with cases of bullying among older students.

Endnotes

1 The phrase "spare the rod and spoil the child" was in fact coined, with satirical intent, by Samuel Butler in the nineteenth century but he doubtless had in mind Proverbs 23:13–14: "Withhold not correction from the child: for [if] thou beatest him with the rod, he shall not die. Thou shalt beat him with the rod, and shalt deliver his soul from hell."

2 The idea that it is right for a person who is injured by another to obtain exact revenge in the form of "an eye for an eye, a tooth for a tooth" was enshrined in the code of Hammurabi, King of Babylon, 1792–1750 BC (Exodus, 21:23–27).

3   Results from an online survey conducted in the United States in 2007 indicated that around 75 percent of teachers believed that the use of punishment was justified when addressing even mild cases of bullying (Bauman *et al.* 2008). The survey, when conducted in a number of other countries including Canada, Australia, Norway, Germany, and Finland, produced comparable results.

4   See Whitted and Dupper (2005).

5   The quotation is taken from a website, posted by Barbara Ling on http://www.barbaraling.com/insights/smashing-bullies-self-confidence. Accessed August 14, 2009.

6   Olweus (1993) discusses rules or guidelines that students may be encouraged to develop through classroom discussion on the subject of bullying.

7   In a case study conducted in England in a secondary school, Mahdavi and Smith (2002) sought judgments from students and teachers about the usefulness of bully courts as a means of addressing cases of bullying. This approach was strongly supported by both students and staff.

8   Indirect or relational forms of bullying were reported as being the most hurtful (compared with direct physical and verbal bullying) by a sample of 14-year-old secondary school students (Rigby & Bagshaw 2001).

9   Pavlov (1849–1936) was a Russian physiologist famous for his explanation of behavior as the outcomes of conditioned reflexes.

10 Depicted in Kubrick's film, *A Clockwork Orange*, based upon the novel by Anthony Burgess (1962).

11 B. F. Skinner (1904–1990) was an influential behavioral psychologist, especially in the 1950s and 1960s. See Skinner (1953).

12 See Olweus (1993).

13 Metzler *et al.* (2001) carried out this highly systematic and detailed study in Oregon in 2001.

14 Social influence according to the social psychologist Kelman (1961) may involve quite different processes. These include compliance – a relatively superficial response to negative or positive reinforcement – and internalization which can occur under conditions in which a person decides what is the right thing to do without being subjected to external pressure.

15 This observation was made by Anthony Storr (1989, p. 272) in a chapter entitled: "Why human beings become violent".

16 See Chapter 7 on Restorative Justice in this book.

17 Stevens *et al.* (2000) implemented the Olweus program in Flanders and reported that the outcome was unsuccessful among secondary students but achieved a measure of success with primary school students.

Chapter 5

Strengthening the Victim

Some teachers and counselors believe that a child can avoid being bullied by learning to become less vulnerable. As a consequence, some schools have adopted a policy or practice that seeks to strengthen the victim in some way so that he or she can cope with the problem, without requiring an intervention by the school to change the bully's behavior directly. If this can be done, two positive outcomes are achieved. The self-esteem of the victim rises (it is likely to fall if the school 'fixes' the problem), and the school need not take action to discipline the bully, thereby avoiding any negative consequences associated with the use of punishment.

Taking steps to solve the problem of bullying by strengthening the victim is controversial. Many teachers are unsure whether it is a good idea. This was evident from a large-scale online survey conducted across a number of countries. About a quarter of the teachers were unsure whether they were prepared to help the victim to 'stand up to the bully'; the rest were about equally divided about whether they would adopt this approach.[1]

Bullying Interventions in Schools: Six Basic Approaches, First Edition. Ken Rigby.
© 2012 Ken Rigby. Published 2012 by Blackwell Publishing Ltd.

The misgivings of some teachers arise because they have in mind cases of bullying where the imbalance of power is large and probably cannot be resolved by efforts that the victim could make. Sometimes educators express the view that the victim is doing his best and if he could resist, he would. Still others believe there are ways in which the victim can be helped to act so as to improve the situation.

The possibility of strengthening the victim arises when it is thought that the victim can learn to defend himself or herself more effectively, given appropriate instruction and guidance. The decision to use this approach will depend in part on an assessment of the situation and the circumstances in which the student is being bullied; for example, whether the bully or bullies are much more powerful than their target and resistance would be difficult or impossible. It will also depend upon an assessment of whether the student could or would acquire the necessary capability to resist effectively. Once it is decided that the victim of school bullying can be helped to offer an effective defense, attention is given to the means by which this can be brought about.

Strategies

Strengthening a victim may sometimes be conceived as a relatively long-term project. Years of being a 'victim' who is unable to stand up to the demands of others cannot be remedied overnight. Such an individual needs to be built up gradually through the acquisition of greater confidence. This entails developing a more positive attitude toward oneself and being more resilient and assertive in relating to others.

Building confidence

One powerful way of bringing about long-term change is through the use of rational emotive education.[2] This approach seeks to develop ways of thinking about oneself that are positive, and to prevent the viewing of unfortunate events as awful catastrophes. It seeks to counter a tendency among some children who are bullied to lose self-esteem or self-acceptance, and become even more vulnerable to those who would bully them. Advice is given to students who are often victimized to enable them to think differently about themselves and the things that happen to them.

More broadly, efforts may be directed toward the development of greater emotional intelligence, especially by getting victimized students to observe closely the behavior of those students who cope well with social difficulties. Emotional intelligence includes the ability to perceive and assess other people's emotions and also the capacity to positively influence one's own and other people's emotions.[3] Here is an example of emotional intelligence in action.

> Three 12-year-olds are heading to a soccer field for gym class. Two athletic-looking boys are walking behind – and snickering at – the third, a somewhat chubby classmate.
>
> "So you're going to *try* to play soccer", one of the two says sarcastically to the third, his voice dripping with contempt.
>
> The chubby boy closes his eyes for a moment and takes a deep breath. Then he turns to the other two and replies, in a calm matter-of-fact voice, "Yeah, I'm going to try – but I'm not very good at it".
>
> After a pause, he adds, "But I'm great at art. Show me something and I can draw it real good...".
>
> Then pointing to his antagonist, he says, "Now you, you're great at soccer – really fantastic! I'd like to be as good some day, I'm just not. Maybe I can get better if I keep trying."
>
> At that, the first boy, his disdain now totally disarmed, says in a friendly tone, "Well, you're not really *that* bad! I can show you a few things about how to play."[4]

It can be helpful to share such examples with vulnerable students. Some practitioners have undertaken the task of directly helping groups of victimized students to acquire more positive attitudes toward themselves and skills to defend themselves against bullying. In a safe environment, students can be taught to try out new ways of behaving that will make them less of a target, for instance, by relating more positively with others and making friends.

Some teachers and counselors choose to work more intensively with a smaller group of students who have been identified as needing help with their social interactions.[5] Such students are invited by a teacher or counselor to a meeting which could help them to make friends and get on with others better. Exercises are devised to help them become more confident and assertive, to say 'no' when unreasonable requests are made of them, and to deal more effectively with those who would bully them. Such work may include teaching basic social skills of the kind that students who are bullied commonly lack, for instance how to introduce oneself, join in with a group, and make friends. These skills are practiced in circumstances in which no one feels threatened.

Typically a number of sessions are needed, beginning with an exercise in which each child makes a positive statement about themselves (not easy for some victimized children to do), and culminating – after training – in demonstrating that hearing abusive language or being threatened can be handled confidently. Games are played to build confidence in interacting with group members, and the capacity to make friends is fostered. With older children especially, group members may be encouraged to talk about difficulties they have had with other students and brainstorm solutions. An important element of these sessions is students reporting back to other members of the group on suggested techniques they have tried and with what success. The success of this work depends largely on the concern, enthusiasm, and sensitivity of the practitioner.

Much has been said about the development of resilience as an antidote to becoming demoralized when things get tough – as they do when one is bullied.[6] Two factors should be recognized in seeking to help students to become more resilient. The first is the provision of social support, for example, through providing supportive mentoring by fellow students or by adult volunteers.[7] Children who feel supported are less likely to feel stressed, are less likely to be bullied, and more able to cope with interpersonal difficulties. The second factor is participating in cooperative ventures. Children who cooperate with others are less likely to become involved in bully/victim problems. Providing the opportunity and incentive for victimized students to take part in cooperative learning is one means of increasing their resilience.[8]

Physical skills

When the means of strengthening the victim are discussed, the teaching of martial arts is often suggested. Some think that having acquired such skills, the victim will be more confident and more capable of defending himself or herself. In some situations, at least, the acquisition of such skills is likely to make you more confident, especially when someone tries to intimidate you physically. The confidence that is acquired may not, however, extend to verbal forms of bullying. When verbally attacked, a verbal form of assertiveness is generally required. It has been pointed out that sometimes acquiring greater physical strength through participating in power sports can have negative effects on interpersonal behavior. There is in fact good evidence that children who engage in such sports as weight lifting, martial arts, boxing, and wrestling are more likely than others to engage in bullying at school.[9] This does not mean that participating in such activities should be discouraged, but rather that care should be taken to ensure that students do not abuse the power they achieve. One useful training course for empowering young people, both physically and mentally, that incorporates a philosophy of nonviolence is the Rock and Water program.[10]

Verbal skills

Alternative ways of defending oneself against verbal bullying have been suggested.[11] One is to 'give it back to the bully'. That is, treat the bully with the same kind of contempt as he or she has shown to you. Mount a verbal counterattack, for example:

BULLY: *You look like a witch.*
TARGET: *That's funny coming from a hag like you.*

In this example, the target is attempting to show (i) that she is not to be intimidated and (ii) she can make a clever and cutting remark that will convince the bully that in a verbal duel she might come off worse. The aim appears to be to show up the bully as being inferior – in the next example, intellectually inferior:

BULLY: *You're an idiot.*
TARGET: *According to psychologists, an idiot has a very low IQ which means I couldn't qualify for this class.*

Whether this mode of responding is generally effective is debatable. It seems likely to inflame matters and, if the victim is less verbally skilled or less confident than the bully, such repartee may actually make matters worse.

Fogging

A safer and more acceptable mode of responding to bullying is known as 'fogging'.[12] This is an assertiveness technique that may be taught to students who are being targeted to assist them in coping with insults and putdowns. It assumes that the bully is motivated to get a rise out of the victim through teasing or taunting. The bully is typically bored and is looking for a response that is entertaining. The bully wants the victim to feel upset, angry, and impotent. If the response of the target is calm and nonchalant, the bully becomes frustrated and is likely to stop – and perhaps seek out a more entertaining victim. Fogging involves the victim doing the opposite to what the bully expects.

This technique avoids directly challenging the bully who is out to tease or taunt the victim; for example the victim might say quite casually: "That's your opinion", or "Could be, possibly" or "You might think so". The point is that the bully gets little or no reaction. Instead of getting into a 'flap' – and thereby encouraging the bullying – the victim reacts unemotionally. The intended insults are swallowed up as in a dense fog.

In cases of mild bullying, this is a useful and practical technique and can result in a de-escalation of a conflict. However, the task in 'taking on' the bully is not an easy one and some training and rehearsing is generally needed before this approach can be confidently and effectively employed. The intended victim needs to stand firm, refuse to be intimidated, and look the bully in the eye. Essentially, the targeted child should act or pretend – if necessary – to be brave. Instead of competing with the bully in being offensive, the intended victim responds in a nonchalant way, acknowledging that what the bully says may be how he or she actually sees things. By focusing on the *perceptions* of the bully, the sting is taken out of what the bully is saying. The words used, however, must be ones that the intended victim is comfortable in using and not necessarily the ones invented by the practitioner.

When the opportunity arises, the bully may be asked to explain why he or she apparently thinks that way about the intended victim. This question can put the bully on the back foot. It is unexpected and disconcerting. It requires the bully to think about his or her behavior. The preparation of the victim for such an encounter with the bully needs to be carefully considered and thorough. It can be useful for the victim to rehearse what might be said with the instructor or with a helpful partner. Helping students to act in an assertive manner requires a good deal of cooperation between the practitioner and the student who is being bullied. The latter is often the best judge of what might 'work' in a given situation. If the practitioner is too directive, the student may be seen as responding in a phony and unnatural way. The detail of what useful responses could be should be worked out in partnership. An exercise is provided in Appendix 2 that illustrates this technique.

Critique

As an approach to countering bullying, strengthening the victim has much to commend it. It avoids having to confront the bully or bullies in order to discipline them – with possible or even probable negative consequences for the victim from recriminatory treatment. Unlike working with bullies who are often resistant to change, victims are commonly highly motivated to try out new ways of dealing with the problem, especially if they see the possibility of success. If the victim is enabled to solve the problem, there is no need for further action on the part of the school. The rise in the erstwhile victim's self-esteem and self-acceptance after taking effective action is highly gratifying. The victim may have acquired both confidence and skill that will be useful in dealing with similar difficulties in years to come.

Yet, as we have seen, this approach is not popular or favored by a good number of teachers. Some objections stem from a belief that the bullies should be disciplined and that, as a rule, the victim is 'doing his best' and in a sense is being blamed for not doing better. A more common questioning of this approach comes from the belief that in many cases it simply will not work; that is, the victim cannot be helped to solve the problem himself or herself. It is asserted that the nature of bullying is such that it occurs essentially in situations in which there is an imbalance of power, often insurmountable. Victims are at a serious disadvantage and – so it is often claimed – would surely solve the problem if they could.

The sensible course is to recognize that cases of bullying differ. In some cases, the odds are stacked hugely against the victim, as when a group of thugs confront a much weaker person who has no power to resist. In other cases, it may be feasible that, with good advice and perhaps some training, the imbalance may be overcome and the tables turned on the tormentors.

Sometimes it is difficult to determine whether strengthening the victim is a viable approach in particular cases. A good assessment is required of the capacity or capability of the victim to benefit from this mode of intervention. The practitioner of this method needs to make a careful appraisal of the current level of vulnerability of the victim, and what can reasonably be expected of the victim, that is, after appropriate training and guidance. This is far from easy.

Vulnerability to bullying may be of different kinds. A student is especially vulnerable if there is something about their appearance and behavior that leads to them being continually attacked. They are vulnerable if they cannot learn how to defend themselves well. A lack of resilience and the inability to 'bounce back' may further increase their vulnerability. In each of these areas, vulnerability is not easy to assess.

The likelihood of being attacked and bullied may require a change in a student's way of behaving with other students, for example, in being able to act assertively and make friends. Some students resist change or find it difficult or impossible to change. Some appear incapable of learning how not to act in a way that brings about unwelcome attention. Some do have an appropriate repertoire of social skills that would serve them well – if only they could be brought to use them when they are being bullied. The question here is: Can they be induced to try?

Judgments must be made largely on an individual case basis. These include disadvantages or limitations that may be physical, psychological, or social. Here is a list of some specific sources of vulnerability.

Physical disadvantage

This may be general, as in being less physically robust than other children; or specific, as in cases of children who have a physical handicap or a sensory weakness, such as defective eyesight or hearing. Such disadvantages as these may attract bullying from children who think they can easily dominate them.

Psychological disadvantage

This includes psychological characteristics which commonly render a child more likely to be attacked by some peers. Some fall within the normal range, such as being relatively introverted, timid, anxious, having poor social skills, and a low level of self-esteem.[13] Low resilience may also result in a child being vulnerable to bullying. For such a person, not only will negative treatment from peers result in more stress, but a display of unusually high reactivity to low degrees of harassment may actually encourage some students to target that person. Other less frequently observed characteristics that generally make a student vulnerable include intellectual disability, autism spectrum disorder (including Asperger syndrome), ADHD, Tourette syndrome, and clinical depression. All these conditions tend to invite aggression from some children and may make it difficult for those targeted to defend themselves.

Social disadvantage

This source of disadvantage may arise as a result of prejudice directed toward an individual because he or she is, or is perceived to be, a member of an unpopular social group, such as an ethnic minority group. Or the prejudice may be related to the way a person behaves, or is thought to behave, as in the case of homophobia. Social disadvantage may also occur as a result of isolation from other students. Sometimes this is due to an inability or unwillingness of a child to make friends and, in a minority of cases, from a tendency toward acting provocatively and seemingly inviting victimization.

The disadvantages experienced by some victimized students do not necessarily mean that they cannot be helped by being strengthened in some way. Take for example children with cognitive deficits, such as children with an intellectual disability, or those who have Asperger syndrome. Children with intellectual disability cannot acquire sophisticated verbal skills that could overwhelm those who might ridicule them. Nevertheless, there are things that can be done to reduce the likelihood of such children being bullied. They can be helped by learning how to suppress strong expressions of anguish when they are teased, and thereby reduce the dubious pleasure that their tormentors might gain and seek repeatedly to obtain.[14] Asperger children can be taught to recognize cues that other children interpret intuitively and thereby avoid dangerous situations.[15]

In some cases, a disadvantageous condition may be temporary and capable of being overcome – and needing to be overcome before much progress can be made in helping a student to act assertively. This is particularly true if the student has become seriously depressed or traumatized by an experience of being bullied. Such conditions must be addressed before it becomes possible for the student to apply the kind of social skills that could prevent the bullying from continuing.

Perhaps the main concern for schools lies in the use of a strengthening technique that is really inappropriate. This – as I have tried to show – can occur if the vulnerability of the victim is not carefully considered. Some techniques with some students can make matters worse, and expose students to greater danger. Hence, considerable care is needed in matching the mode of strengthening the victim with the condition and capability of the victim. The biggest danger seems to be in urging students to respond to verbal bullying in an offensive or supersmart way, so as to antagonize the bully further. Techniques that seek to build up the confidence and social skills – and especially the social intelligence – of victims can be very helpful. When taught carefully, techniques such as 'fogging' can benefit many children.

It should not be assumed that adopting a sensible method of strengthening a given victim is to be recommended to the exclusion of other approaches. It can be used in a complementary way to other methods. For instance, sanctions may be applied to deter further bullying, and strengthening the victim may be important in those cases where the traditional disciplinary approach is not entirely effective. Strengthening the victim is compatible with other approaches as well – as we shall see.

The Future

It has often been said that bullying can only occur when there is an imbalance of power between potential bullies and potential victims. Nevertheless, it may be pointed out that power imbalances between people are rarely fixed and may sometimes be quite fluid. The puny guy who gets sand kicked in his face and goes away to get 'muscled up' and 'beats up' the bully is not entirely mythical. But an imbalance of power is much more likely to be bridged – if bridgeable – by the acquisition of relevant social skills, a growth in confidence, and through the support of friends. To some extent – and in some situations – the school can help in this regard, and can be expected to focus more and more on this method of intervention.

Suggestions about how children can act more assertively and solve their own problems are constantly being made. What I think, and hope, will happen is that suggestions will increasingly be evaluated by teachers and sensible judgments will be made about the circumstances in which they are likely to be effective, or conversely make matters worse for the victim. Currently, there is an air of unreality about when and how vulnerable children can be helped to help themselves. We still await the appearance of research that will shed some light on which methods of strengthening victims against bullying actually work. Finally, as schools become aware of the variety of intervention approaches that can be used in particular situations, it seems likely that working with and 'strengthening the victim' will be used to complement other methods. As a method to be used on its own, in *all* situations, it is sadly inadequate. Used thoughtfully with or without other forms of intervention, it can be very useful.

Endnotes

1   In an online survey conducted by Bauman *et al.* (2008) of 736 US teachers and counselors, some 36 percent of respondents thought that they would "tell the victim to stand up to the bully"; 40 percent thought they would not; and 24 percent were uncertain.

2   Based upon the rational emotive theory of Albert Ellis (1961), a South Australian counselor, Giulio Bortolozzi (see www.haveagospaghettio.com.au), has developed a teaching program designed to help children to become more self-accepting.

3   The exploration of the nature of emotional intelligence has been undertaken by Goleman (1995) whose work is particularly helpful in suggesting how this quality can be developed in children.

4   The example demonstrating emotional intelligence is reproduced with permission from Goleman (2006/2007).

5   Working with victimized children has been a feature of the group work undertaken by the English authority on school bullying, Sonia Sharp. An account of this work is given in Rigby and Sharp (1993).

6   McGrath and Noble (2003) have provided a program for schools aimed at increasing student resilience.

7   The mentors in this case reported by King *et al.* (2002) were adults recruited from the community and trained to mentor Year 4 students who had been identified as children whose behavior placed them 'at risk' of being psychologically or physically harmed. Over a 12-month period, significant improvement in the mental health of these children was observed.

8 Readiness to engage in cooperative work with other children at school has been found to be less common among victimized students (Rigby *et al.* 1997). Much pioneering work in the area of cooperative learning has been undertaken by Johnson *et al.* (1993) in the United States and by Helen Cowie *et al.* (1994) in England, especially in relation to bullying.

9 Endressen and Olweus (2005) have reported that students who participate in power sports are significantly more likely than others to engage in bullying at school.

10 The Rock and Water program aims at developing in students over the age of nine years a sense of physical and psychological confidence through engagement in physical and interactive exercises. See Ykema (2002).

11 Examples of the kinds of things children can say when somebody tries to bully them are provided in a book by Evelyn Field (1999).

12 See www.nbt.nhs.uk/services/surgery/cleftlippalate/documents/Inform ation%20suitable%20for%20direct%20access%20from%20website/ Bullying%20and%20Teasing/Bully%20Busting.pdf for information about fogging on which the exercise in Appendix 2 is, in part, based.

13 The association between low self-esteem and being victimized at school has been examined in a number of studies, for example, by Egan and Perry (1998) among young children, and Rigby and Slee (1993) among adolescents.

14 Nettelbeck and Wilson (2002) have reported that although young people with intellectual disability are more vulnerable to peer victimization than others, with training they may learn to control their angry reactions to teasing and become much less affected by negative treatment.

15 Vulnerability to bullying at school among Asperger children is discussed at length by Dubin (2007) who suggests ways in which these children can be helped.

Chapter 6

Mediation

Mediation as a means of intervention in cases of conflict between students may be seen as a reaction against traditional forms of intervention which seek to impose solutions to problems in an authoritative or authoritarian manner, rather than assist the protagonists to find a solution for themselves. Originating in the United States in the 1960s, the mediation approach has spread to many countries around the world, including Canada, England, and Australia. It is practiced in an increasing number of schools, more commonly in primary and middle school, but also, less often, in secondary schools. Its application to cases of bullying is relatively new and, as we shall see, is still controversial.

Broadly, mediation is an attempt to bring about a peaceful settlement or compromise between disputants through the intervention of a neutral party. It is distinct from arbitration, which is sometimes carried out in schools when students in conflict accept the verdict of a third party (a teacher or counselor) as to how the conflict is to be resolved. With mediation the protagonists enter into negotiation with each other freely – that is without compulsion – and are assisted by a trained mediator to reach an agreed and peaceful solution.

Bullying Interventions in Schools: Six Basic Approaches, First Edition. Ken Rigby.
© 2012 Ken Rigby. Published 2012 by Blackwell Publishing Ltd.

The mediator may be an adult, usually a member of staff who has received some professional training in the method, or a student who has received some relevant training at the school. The latter are known as peer mediators. There are advantages in mediation being done by students. They do not generally come over as 'authority figures' and are less likely than teachers to impose their will on proceedings. Moreover, students are more likely to understand the situations in which their fellow students find themselves. Hence mediation is commonly carried out by students with students.

The main distinguishing features of mediation are as follows:[1]

- Disputants retain power over the process and outcomes.
- The parties define the conflict and are encouraged, with the assistance of the mediator, to resolve the dispute themselves.
- Mediators are impartial and do not 'take sides'.
- Mediators do not discipline anyone: they act nonpunitively.
- Mediators do not act as arbitrators, that is, they do not give their opinions or make judgments about who is right.
- Participation is entirely voluntary.
- The disputants are free to leave if they feel that the process is not helpful to them.
- The process is future oriented, that is, concerned with producing a mutually acceptable outcome.

Mediation sometimes takes place 'on the spot' in the schoolyard or classroom by peer mediators or teachers, in situations in which the contending parties are agreeable to receive help to resolve a difference or dispute. Alternatively, the mediation may be conducted later in private.

Mediation can only begin when individuals in a school have been appropriately trained. Unfortunately, training in conflict resolution and mediation is rarely provided in mainstream preservice training for teachers anywhere in the world, and only occasionally as an elective. However, some organizations can be accessed to provide professional training (for instance, in Australia it can be provided by the Australian Education Union). The training of students in conflict management and peer mediation is sometimes carried out as part of the school curriculum, in which case every student may receive instruction. More often, however, training is directed toward a group of students who may be selected according to various criteria. Teachers may choose students who appear to have appropriate qualities, for example, good listening and communication skills. They may be identified as potential leaders. Alternatively, they may be elected by their fellow students, chosen randomly or selected so as to represent a diversity of demographic or personal characteristics. Those chosen might form a 'cadre' and receive training at intervals (sometimes weekly) from a trained mediator. These sessions are generally conducted outside of the regular curriculum, during lunch time or after school. The training ideally includes supervised practice. Once a system of training peer mediators has become established, the students who have been trained and have practiced their skills may instruct a new cohort of trainees.

Typically mediation involves the following stages:

1. Identifying students who are in conflict and are ready to negotiate, with the help of a mediator, to resolve their differences peaceably. Without such an initial commitment mediation cannot proceed.

2. A meeting is arranged with the students who are in conflict. Although some mediation may be attempted 'on the spot' by a mediator who happens to encounter children who are at odds with each other and want to be helped to resolve their problem, more commonly the meeting is held later when tempers have cooled. Generally a private place is found where there will be no interruptions, and the participants meet there.

3. The participants are required to agree to certain rules that make the process of mediation practicable. These include a requirement that only one person talks at a time while the other person listens without interrupting, and that each of them stay to hear each other out.

4. The mediator asks each member to describe in turn what has been happening. The other person must repeat what has been said without making any judgment or comment. The mediator may prompt, if necessary, to seek more information, and clarify what is being said. Importantly, at this stage there is to be no discussion or point-scoring.

5. While the participants describe what they see as having happened, the mediator must listen carefully, and then summarize what has been said to the satisfaction of those involved.

6. Having established what happened according to the participants, the next stage is to enable the speakers to share their feelings about each other's actions. Again each of them is expected to say how they felt without being interrupted and the other to reflect back what has been said – without making any comment. Again the mediator summarizes what has been said.

7. Next, the mediator invites the participants to make suggestions about what could be done to improve matters and these are listed.

8. Having a list of options before them, the participants are then invited to choose a solution to the conflict that is most acceptable to them. This may involve the participants in finding a win–win course of action that effectively solves the problem, or they may agree to a compromise. It is not up to the mediator to say which solution is best.

9. The mediator records what the parties have agreed upon, using their own words, and each of them is expected to sign a document to indicate that they will abide by the agreement.

10. Subsequently, the behavior of the participants is monitored and, if necessary, further meetings may be held.

Figure 6.1   Peer mediation. From Lewers and Murphy (2000, p. 61). © Curriculum Corporation. Reproduced with permission of Education Services Australia, www.esa.edu.au.

In practice, there may be some variation in how mediation is carried out. For instance, some schools have sought to mediate between students AFTER the offender has been disciplined. There are also schools in which children who have bullied others are given the option of being disciplined or accepting mediation. Some schools hold the threat of punishment over the 'offender' if he or she does not cooperate. It must be emphasized that these applications are inconsistent with the generally accepted philosophy of mediation, which requires that those in dispute are treated impartially, nonjudgmentally, and helped to reach a solution that is no way forced or part of a process that implies coercion or manipulation (Figure 6.1).

Critique

It is generally accepted that mediation is difficult, if not impossible, to achieve if there is a notable imbalance of power between the bully and the victim. Typically the bully is satisfied with the current situation.

The victim is being dominated, as intended; quite possibly the bully is being admired by some others; in some schools high status is being achieved or sustained. For the bully, there may be little or nothing to be gained from ending the conflict, and something to lose. The victim on the other hand may have much to gain, especially freedom from oppression. In such a situation it is difficult, if not impossible, for the person taking the role of the mediator to remain impartial.

This is a serious problem that mediators must face. It raises the practical issue of how a mediator can help to bring about an agreed solution between the bully and the victim, when the bully has the power to insist upon an outcome that is not acceptable to the victim. Bear in mind that the mediator is committed to taking a neutral stance and cannot redress the balance by favoring the victim. The problem is much more difficult to handle if the imbalance of power between them is large and stable, and if there is no provocation on the part of the victim that could make for possible concessions or compromises by both parties. Provocation on the part of victims is relatively rare.

Not surprisingly, some schools are particularly opposed to supporting mediation in dealing with cases of bullying where the bullying has been severe and the perpetrator(s) is seen as highly culpable. It may in fact be difficult to find members of staff or students who are prepared to mediate in such circumstances. This means that mediation tends to be limited to cases of low severity or cases in which there is relatively little imbalance of power.

In some schools, students show a strong interest in becoming peer mediators and finding students to be trained is not a problem. In other schools, however, there may be considerable difficulties in finding and keeping together a group of students to receive the training and then practice the art of mediating. Two American researchers[2] have provided a disturbing account of factors that inhibit the use of peer mediation in one junior high school. Some 74 percent of students at the school thought that student attitudes toward mediation were a major deterrent to its use. Many distrusted the process, fearing that they would be ridiculed if they asked mediators for help and thought that the peer mediators would not respect confidentiality. Many students felt that conflicts should be resolved by force. This observation is consistent with one judgment made of how boys feel when they are in conflict with a peer:

> Fighting is the only way some students know how to maintain their dignity, win the respect of peers, or be successful.[3]

In some schools, perceived norms are such that students feel obliged to fight and reject negotiation as a soft option. This suggests that changes in the school climate or ethos may sometimes need to be made before peer mediation becomes a practical proposition, especially among young teenage boys.

Objections to peer mediation are sometimes raised by parents, partly because they want to see the person who bullied their child punished rather than 'mediated with'. They may also suspect that the mediation process will not be well carried out. They suspect that practitioners will be fooled by bullies who manipulate them and lead them to believe that a viable solution has been freely reached when it has not.

A further problem that may arise relates to the quality of the training that students receive and the maturity of the trainees. Without careful training and supervision, a peer mediator or 'peacekeeper' may flounder or misperceive their role. At one primary school I visited I was told: "The peacekeepers … were turning into little Hitlers, for instance yelling 'Get out of there – you know you shouldn't be there.' They have blue shirts. Parents think it's wonderful but teachers think it's legitimised bullying."[4]

Despite the misgivings sometimes expressed by critics of peer mediation, there is some evidence that with good training mediation can be effective in reducing some negative forms of conflict in schools; for example, there is positive evidence from the peer mediators.[5] Success rates of 58 percent to 93 percent have been reported at various sites, where success was measured by whether an agreement was reached and maintained at the time of a follow-up evaluation.[6] It is not always evident, however, what constitutes success. In some studies, 'success' is indicated when the protagonists agree to avoid each other.[7] The evidence from a recent longitudinal study of the effectiveness of peer counseling involving mediation in reducing bullying suggests that it may help to raise the self-esteem of the counselors, but has no significant effect on the level of bullying in a school.[8] The evidence thus appears inconclusive. It appears that the greater the proportion of students involved in mediating conflicts, the greater will be the positive effects on the mental health of students in a school. Under those conditions, one would expect that some cases of bullying would be easier to resolve.

There are two notable factors that affect the success of mediation. One is the quality of the training that is provided, to which reference has already been made. But even when instructors are well trained themselves – and as we have seen very few teachers receive relevant preservice training – the time allocated to teaching about conflict resolution and mediation is often limited to ensure that traditional school topics are covered. This is despite the fact that there is no evidence that allocating time for such skill development jeopardizes academic achievement. This means that practice in the use of mediation skills may be sacrificed, which severely limits the usefulness of the instruction. In addition, time and resources are required to monitor the application of peer mediation and to provide support for the mediators. This is not always seen as practicable.

The second factor is the contribution of the school ethos in influencing the readiness of students to be trained as mediators and to find students who are prepared to be mediated. It has been argued that the mediation approach is unlikely to work in schools that are not ready for it and that a change in how the school operates is a necessary precursor. Where authoritarian structures predominate and teachers exercise rigid control over student behavior, invariably using punitive methods in dealing with cases of bullying, the practice of mediation is harder to introduce and gain acceptance. On the other hand, once cases of conflict have been dealt with successfully through mediation, the school ethos itself begins to change. The relationship between the prevailing school ethos and the success of new ways of resolving conflict is reciprocal.

Some Conclusions

We must now return to the problem of how mediation can directly affect bullying. As we have seen, bullying in which there is a substantial imbalance of power is difficult or impossible to tackle using mediation methods. Hence the scope of application is limited. Some suggestions have been made to address the problem of power imbalance. One is to allow the victim to bring a friend into the mediation session. This may be helpful. But arguably, it is sending a message to the bully that things are being arranged to pressure him or her into making a compromise or accepting a solution. Some would argue that in fact this is departing from the spirit of mediation. Another suggestion is to use a mediation process after students have already made progress through discussions with a counselor to a point at which an imbalance of power is no longer relevant. This is a feature of the Method of Shared Concern, to be discussed later.

I conclude that direct applications of mediation to cases of bullying are much more likely to be successful in some circumstances than others. These include those in which the practitioners, whether students or staff, are well trained and aware of the strengths and limitations of the approach. A school environment that provides strong support for its use is needed. Generally, one would expect cases of bullying to be resolved using this method more readily when the imbalance of power between the students in conflict is relatively small and there is a readiness on the part of the students to seek an uncoerced resolution of the problem. Judging from the fact that some investigators have not found significant reductions in bullying following the use of a mediation process, it may be wise to limit the area in which mediation is used. Given the right circumstances and the appropriate selection of cases, there are grounds for expecting the method to be helpful in reducing bullying.

Endnotes

1   This is, in part, adapted from a highly helpful book by Richard Cohen (2005), *Students Resolving Conflict: Peer Mediation in Schools*.

2   See Theberge and Karan (2004).

3   See Curwin (1995, p. 72).

4   This comment was made to me in the course of collecting data for an account of the views of Australian counselors on what was being done in Australian schools to counter bullying. See Rigby and Thomas (2003, p. 31).

5   In a study of the work of 15 Year 5 mediators in a school in England, Cremin (2002) reported that all of them indicated publicly that they had conducted at least one successful intervention and that 8 of them had been 'frequently successful'.

6   These estimates were provided by several pioneers in the use of peer resolution methods in US schools, Johnson *et al.* (1992).

7   Johnson and Johnson (1996) have reported that the most common outcome of mediation between students in conflict is that they agree to avoid each other in future.

8   In a one year longitudinal study at an all-girls secondary school in England where peer counselors were active, there was no evidence that the level of school bullying was reduced. There were, however, significant improvements in the social self-esteem of the students who had been trained as peer counselors at the school (Houlston & Smith 2009).

Chapter 7

Restorative Justice

Restorative Justice and restorative practice are terms that are often used interchangeably. However, it is useful to view Restorative Justice as describing the more general or philosophic nature of a movement that employs various procedures to achieve a just outcome. Restorative practice refers more specifically to the procedures that are employed in achieving Restorative Justice.

The application of restorative practices in dealing with cases of school bullying has become increasingly popular in schools, especially over the last 10 years. Like mediation, Restorative Justice is often seen as a reaction against traditional disciplinary means of dealing with conflict between students. However, let us not overstate the contrast. Firstly, it is well to recognize that the traditional disciplinary approach is also commonly concerned with justice, that is, acting in a fair and even-handed manner; and secondly, the approach we call Restorative Justice also puts pressure on the offender to change in what the school authorities believe is a desirable direction. The differences are important but rather more subtle.

The charge often made against traditional disciplinary approaches is that they are retributive; they require that the perpetrator suffers

Bullying Interventions in Schools: Six Basic Approaches, First Edition. Ken Rigby.
© 2012 Ken Rigby. Published 2012 by Blackwell Publishing Ltd.

because he or she has made the victim suffer. It is true that some disciplinarians think that way but some do not. Many of them are concerned not with exacting revenge, but rather producing a change in the behavior of the perpetrator. Both the traditional approach and that of Restorative Justice are prepared to put pressure on the perpetrator to bring about a desired change.

Restorative Justice and the traditional disciplinary approach have something more in common. They are alike in rejecting the purely mediational approach. Neither adopts a neutral stance in dealing with the children who are in conflict. They do not treat the bully and the victim alike. They expect the bully to change. Far from being neutral, they are both quite directive.

So how do they differ? An essential difference was brought home to me in discussion with a secondary school principal with whom I had a disagreement. We had been listening to an account of how another teacher had handled a case of bullying, seemingly pretty effectively, in that the bullies (two boys) had sincerely apologized and agreed to be friends with the boy they had been treating badly. A satisfactory conclusion, I thought. The principal did not agree. The two boys must be warned that any more of it and they would be severely punished. As we talked further I began to understand why we differed. As he put it, the important thing in dealing with bullies is the nature of the relationship that you (the school authority) have with them. They must be brought to realize that they cannot win. They need to be brought under control. They must be in a state in which they DARE not re-offend. I said, perhaps a little too heatedly, that I thought that the really important thing was the relationship between the two boys and the boy they had bullied. And further that the role of the teacher was that of a facilitator who had brought about this minor miracle. We begged to differ.

The essence of Restorative Justice is to bring about good or tolerable relationships when things have gone wrong. It is not just to control the bad guys who have offended against the school, having broken the 'reasonable rules' that have been put in place. It is more than that. It also seeks to heal the hurt that has occurred; to put it behind the offender. It is essentially future oriented.

Restorative Practice

Restorative practice may take a variety of forms.[1] They may involve a relatively informal meeting with the bully (designated as the 'wrongdoer') often with the victim present; there may be, on occasions, others also present, for instance a number of other students, sometimes a whole class. Much more formally, a so-called community conference may be convened at which the bully and the victim are both present, together with other interested persons such as the parents and friends of each of the parties. A trained facilitator would run such a meeting.

How a practitioner may work on cases of bullying has been indicated in a procedure described in a number of websites.[2] In some schools, teachers carry about with them a set of cards with printed instructions which set out how cases may be addressed. In the presence of the victim, the bully or 'wrongdoer' may be asked the following questions:[3]

> What happened?
> What were you thinking of at the time?
> What have you thought about since?
> Who has been affected by what you have done? In what way?

The practitioner may now switch to the victim:

> What did you think when you realized what had happened?
> What have you thought about since?
> What impact has this incident had on you and others?
> What has been the hardest thing for you?
> What do you think needs to happen to make things right?

Next, it is back to the wrongdoer:

> What do you think you need to do to make things right?
> How can we make sure this does not happen again?

After a restorative action has been suggested, undertaken, and (importantly) accepted by the target, the case may be concluded, though the situation may continue to be monitored.

Such a detailed scripted approach is often appreciated by teachers as it provides some guidance and structure in dealing with cases. With younger children – in kindergarten or early primary school – the practitioner may be more directive, for instance by stating "At this school it is not okay to … ". And "If the same situation happens again, how could you behave differently?" The offender may be further instructed in how to make an appropriate apology and the one offended against how to respond positively.

In some cases, it is considered appropriate to apply restorative practices in a larger group setting. This is likely to occur when other individuals or groups are involved in the problem, for example, when the issue is one in which a class of children are implicated and their views are relevant to a successful resolution of the problem. In such a case, a meeting is held involving all the students in a class, including those who have not participated in the bullying in any way. The principles however remain the same. The wrongdoer(s) and the victim(s) are encouraged to speak and explain how they have felt about their experiences. How the others respond is of crucial importance. The expectation is that the reactions and views of the listeners will exert pressure on the bully or bullies who will feel remorseful and act restoratively. In no way is such a meeting intended to resemble a trial. However, a message is sent to those who have bullied someone that their behavior is reprehensible and that restorative action is desirable – and if this happens it will meet with the approval of the wider group.

Where the situation is one in which the offense has been particularly serious and there are many who have a stake in how the matter is resolved, a so-called community conference may be held. The nature of the conference is described as follows by the National Centre for Restorative Justice in Education in England:

> [This is a] process which seeks to repair the harm done to relationships within a community by allowing everyone involved to meet and gain a better understanding from each other of the impact of an incident, the reasons for it and the preferred outcomes. The process usually involves

the 'victim' and their parents/supporters and the 'offender' and their supporters as well as key school personnel and behaviour support staff where applicable.[4]

The intention is to promote a comprehensive understanding of what has happened on the part of 'everyone' – the offender, the 'victim', and the interested parties – and restore peace and harmony.

Needless to say, the effectiveness of such a meeting depends in part on the work done 'behind the scenes' in contacting and preparing the participants for the conference.

Basic to this procedure is providing the victim(s) with an opportunity to speak out about the distress that has been experienced at a meeting at which 'justice' is to be achieved with the support of community members. The offender listens. In such circumstances, it is anticipated that he or she will be moved to feel and express remorse, and moreover to indicate what can be done to put things right. The role of those present is to consider and accept whatever apologies and restorative acts are forthcoming.

Understandably such meetings can be intensely emotional and it is possible that some people present may be vindictive and unforgiving. The role of the facilitator is obviously not easy. An outcome must be contrived in which

1. The feelings of those offended against – the victim(s) – are forcefully expressed.
2. The offender (s) – the bully or bullies – and supporters (if any) are chastened and motivated to act restoratively.
3. There is a sincere acceptance by those present of the student who has offended and everyone is ready to move on.

Critique

There is no doubt that Restorative Justice is a movement that has a strong contemporary appeal and that it is being embraced by an increasing number of schools, for example, in Australia, the United States, Canada, England, and New Zealand. Resource books and websites are now readily available to provide instructions on how it can be employed in schools. It is being welcomed especially by educators who recognize the limitations of the traditional disciplinary approach and at the same time recognize the importance of traditional values, such as justice for victims and forgiveness for those who repent. It accords with a Christian philosophy that seeks to differentiate between the sin and the sinner. The focus is upon the behavior that is bad, not the individual, and the aim is to bring about a change in the way the offender relates to others.

There is nevertheless considerable controversy over both the theory and practice of restorative justice. Much of it focuses on the role of shame in the process. For some psychologists, the emotion of shame has a very negative function. For example, it has been claimed by an eminent prison psychologist that shame is "the primary or ultimate cause of all violence" and that "I have yet to see a serious act of violence that was not provoked by the experience of feeling shamed and humiliated, disrespected and ridiculed."[5]

In reply, it is argued that shame is an emotion that arises naturally with the realization that one has offended, and is a necessary precursor to taking action to alleviate or reduce the harm that has been done. At the same time, it is generally acknowledged that disapproval directed toward the person of the offender is not helpful. Indeed it is recognized that it could be harmful and jeopardize the outcome of the intervention. Hence, distinction is commonly made between undesirable shame that is stigmatizing and desirable shame that is reintegrative. Reintegrative shaming has been defined as "disapproval that is respectful of the person, is terminated by forgiveness and does not label the person as evil."[6]

The question practitioners of Restorative Justice in schools always need to answer is how to ensure that the shaming is reintegrative and not stigmatizing. When a sense of shame or remorse (to use a generally more acceptable term) is already present in the bully, as is sometimes the case, there is no problem. It is pointless and perhaps counterproductive to apply pressure. The script is likely to work like a dream. The child reflects upon his or her feelings and is encouraged to act to remove the pain of feeling bad about what has been done by apologizing and acting restoratively. The victim is encouraged to accept the apology and the issue is resolved. The problem arises when the bully does not naturally feel shame and needs to do so before any progress can be made.

Pressure can take different forms. I have witnessed misuses of the procedure in which two teachers harangued and shouted at a small child who was reluctant to acknowledge that he had inflicted harm on another child. "How do you think … felt when you did that to him?" they yelled. Fortunately such gross misapplications appear to be rare. But it is not always realized that the pressure to feel shame and even stigmatization can be present when a child is surrounded by people who strongly deplore what the child has done and, in some cases, are not particularly respectful. Thoughtful and sustained work is needed to prepare all those who are present to convey to the wrongdoer that it is the bad behavior that is being deplored and not the individual. Under these conditions, the pressure is much more likely to have a constructive outcome.

Difficulties are likely to arise if the application of restorative practice is combined with the use of punishment, as is sometimes the case. For example, one prominent exponent of restorative practice in schools[7] has written: "… some form of punishment may be agreed upon as an outcome of a restorative process" (p. 335). In placing the settlement of the problem in the hands of a community group, this is always a possibility and may undermine the prospects of a successful resolution.

Rightly, the exponents of restorative practice emphasize the importance of the relationship between the offender and all those who have been offended. It is assumed that the wrongdoer will want to become reintegrated in the community which he or she values. Otherwise, the wrongdoer will feel alienated and long for acceptance. In some cultures this assumption can be made with confidence, for example, among the Navaho of North America:

> When members of the Navaho nation try to explain why people harm them, they say that a person who does harm to another acts as if he has no relatives, that is the offending person has become so disconnected

from the world around him, so disconnected from the people he lives and works with each day, that his acts no longer have a personal foundation.[8]

Unfortunately this situation no longer parallels the society in which most of us live. With rare exceptions, the vast bulk of people who constitute the school community do not look compassionately upon the one who has strayed, as do – or did – the Navaho and the Maori. We now live in a splintered society with multiple allegiances. Bullies by and large have their support groups. The school authorities constitute a group that is often perceived by students as irrelevant to their social and emotional needs. So too are some groups of students who do not share the values or lifestyle of those involved in bullying. The typical bully is not an outsider in the sense of being alienated from all other students. As numerous researchers into children's relationships have pointed out, children who bully others are commonly not bereft of friends (though we may reasonably conclude that they are of the 'wrong sort'); indeed in many schools they are popular, much more so than their victims.

Part of the error or misperception of some supporters of Restorative Justice derives from an undue focus on exceptional hate crimes. Such a case was the tragedy of the Virginia Technical College student, Seung-Hui Cho, who in 2007 killed 32 people and wounded many others before finally committing suicide. This affair was widely regarded as a consequence of his becoming severely alienated following repeated rejection and ridicule from his peers at school. Whether such an act of desperation could be called 'bullying' is debatable, but the motivation to bully is often understood as deriving from a similar situation, that is, one of extreme alienation – and quite often this is not so. Children who bully are frequently far from alienated. Indeed, it is their very 'embeddedness' in a sustaining social group that often makes much bullying possible and – depending on the kind of group they are in – sometimes likely. It is often assumed that a sense of belongingness comes exclusively from belonging to a group that is good and compassionate. The norms from such a group are seen as impelling one toward considerate and kindly behavior. But many students belong to groups that are far less admirable. Many children bully because such behavior is expected of them by their friends – sometimes enthusiastically, sometimes reluctantly.

Like many new or newish movements restorative practice attracts 'true believers'. They are individuals who see with great clarity the shortcomings of a strictly punitive and retributive approach that can indeed make matters worse. Unfortunately, they can take a somewhat arrogant and stigmatizing view of people who are critical of the approach they favor and reluctant to embrace it. Individuals who are skeptical of the introduction of restorative practice in a school may be seen as deliberately obstructive. One advocate of restorative practice[9] has described these skeptics as follows:

> The sceptics are just waiting for a reason to NOT come on board. They are waiting for an excuse and as soon as one of your plans does not go smoothly they will jump on the opportunity to spread dissent amongst the ranks.

Other advocates of restorative practice have described these skeptics as 'laggards'.[10] Their recalcitrance is seen as being due to a number of deplorable motives. These include hanging out for retirement; needing to move on some time ago, but fearful of making the change; feeling unsupported by the organization in the past and having been overlooked for promotion; and angry about the fact that they have more experience than others.

How effective has restorative practice proved to be in addressing cases of bullying? From time to time, notably successful applications are reported, as in this one provided by the Restorative Justice Consortium:

> A 15 year old schoolboy took a drug overdose because he was so depressed and intimidated by bullying he was suffering at school. He had been bullied by two brothers in the year above him over several months. They had been hitting him, ripping his uniform, calling him names, spitting at him and threatening violence. The conference gave a voice to everyone involved, and both the boy's story and that of his family had a huge impact on the bullies and their family. The bullies showed true remorse, crying when they realised the harm they had caused. At the end of the conference, an agreement was drawn up. The boys all agreed to look out for each other, and staff arranged to support all the boys.[11]

However, systematic evaluations of the effectiveness of restorative practices have been patchy and usually not rigorous. Although there have been favorable reports obtained from participants in the process, so far there is little evidence of its capacity to produce overall reductions in school bullying. In reviewing the effects of Community Conferences on student behavior, the Youth Justice Board for England and Wales concluded that "to date, there has been little empirical research to demonstrate that restorative justice conferences in schools is effective".[12]

In one major study,[13] the effects of restorative practices in reducing bullying in schools were examined in 26 schools and compared with changes in control schools. No significant differences were found in 23 of the comparisons. There were three comparisons that favored the restorative justice interventions. These were ones that were carried out over a longer period (three years), possibly indicating that the method requires a long-term commitment to be effective. In reporting their findings, the authors pointed out that in about half of these schools the staff knew little or nothing about restorative justice; those who did often had significant misperceptions.

It has been pointed out that implementation of restorative practices in schools is often hindered by tensions between those who are applying restorative principles and those who support a traditional disciplinary approach, typically one involving punishment. Restorative practices need to be embedded in a positive and congruent cultural milieu. Restorative justice remains an attractive possibility; one which may well be effective when it is practiced over a period of several years in the context of a whole school approach that has strong staff and community support.

The Future

The appeal of restorative practice as an alternative to the traditional disciplinary approach favored by most schools is, as we have seen, quite strong. Moreover, the advocates of the method are often well organized and persuasive. In simplifying the process through the use of scripts which tell teachers how to proceed with cases of bullying, the proponents have often been effective in popularizing the method.

Unfortunately, at a theoretical level there is sometimes much confusion and uncertainty about the role that is played by feelings of shame and what steps should be taken to prevent it from being stigmatizing. For some practitioners the concept of shame has been abandoned; sometimes the term 'remorse' is substituted. Hopefully greater clarity will emerge in providing an agreed rationale for the practice.

Progress in effectively implementing restorative practice is being hampered by opposition from some schools where many teachers prefer a strong disciplinary approach. Like some other methods, broad institutional commitment is needed from the relevant educational authority, strong leadership within schools, and adequate training being provided to practitioners. In fact, there often needs to be a transformative culture change in a school that is supportive of the method before it can operate well.

In my view progress will, and should, be made in increasing the application of restorative practices in cases where the facts relating to bullying incidents are clear and acknowledged by everyone; and the person or persons who have bullied feel remorse and are ready to accept guidance as to how they will behave, that is, restoratively. These cases are quite numerous and are still needlessly treated in some schools as requiring punishment. But there are many other cases which are not so easy to treat using restorative practices. These include cases in which the perpetrators do not acknowledge their culpability and do not readily experience a sense of shame. This is more likely to occur when the bullying is in response to a provocation and when their bullying behavior is supported by a group or gang of peers to whom they owe primary allegiance. In conclusion, the problem of how to apply 'reintegrative shaming' in appropriate cases, that is, without stigmatizing the bully, is one that will need to be taken much more seriously.

Endnotes

1   For a comprehensive and practical account of how restorative practices may be used in schools in addressing bullying, see Thorsborne and Vinegrad (2006).

2 See especially www.realjustice.org. For information about useful resources to implement restorative practices see www.circlespeak.com.au.

3 The questions here have been adapted from O'Connell *et al.* (1999) and the full conference facilitator's script can be viewed at www.realjustice.org/Pages/Script.html.

4 For further information about the work of this center see www.transformingconflict.org.

5 See Gilligan (1996, p. 110) for this judgment. Arguably Gilligan had in mind the use of highly stigmatizing procedures.

6 This definition was provided by John Braithwaite (1989), widely regarded as the leading theoretician in the area of restorative justice.

7 Wendy Drewery (2004), a New Zealand authority on restorative practices, sees the use of punishment as not incompatible with some applications of this approach.

8 According to Sullivan and Tifft (2006, p. 1), from whom the quotation was taken, the practice of Restorative Justice is commonly seen as much more acceptable in some communities, such as the Navaho, than others.

9 K. Ferris (2003), a strong advocate of restorative practices, reflecting on the behavior of its critics. http://kmfadvance.server101.com/publication_cultural_revolution.htm.

10 These judgments were made by two prominent exponents of restorative practices, Blood and Thorsborne (2006), in explaining the resistance sometimes experienced in getting restorative justice widely accepted in schools.

11 This example of the success of an application of restorative practice was reproduced with permission from an account given on www.restorativejustice.org.uk. Accessed May 21, 2008.

12 See the Youth Justice Board for England and Wales. National evaluation of the Restorative Justice in schools program (2004). See p. 12. http://www.yjb.gov.uk/Publications/Resources/Downloads/nat%20ev%20of%20rj%20in%20schoolsfullfv.pdf.

13 As reported by two prominent supporters of Restorative Justice, Sherman and Strang (2007, p. 53).

Chapter 8

The Support Group Method
(Formerly the No Blame Approach)

Like the approach taken by the practitioners of restorative practices, the Support Group Method, as devised by Maines and Robinson,[1] is highly critical of a traditional disciplinary approach in which the use of punishment plays a central part.

As with restorative practice, emphasis is placed upon getting the bullies to appreciate the suffering they have inflicted on their victim. Again it is similar to Restorative Justice in that its prime focus is upon providing a solution to the problem rather than providing retribution for a wrongdoing. However there are important differences.

First, the Support Group Method does not assume that a state of shame or remorse on the part of a 'wrongdoer' is a necessary precondition for a positive change in the behavior of those who have engaged in bullying. Hence, according to this view, there are no grounds for seeking to bring about such a state of mind in the perpetrator if none already exists. In place of 'reintegrative shame' as the motivating force that can bring about a positive change in behavior, the practitioners of the Support Group Method posit the development of empathy toward the person who has been hurt.

Bullying Interventions in Schools: Six Basic Approaches, First Edition. Ken Rigby.
© 2012 Ken Rigby. Published 2012 by Blackwell Publishing Ltd.

True to its origins as a so-called No Blame Approach, the Support Group Method does not view the bully as a 'wrongdoer' who needs to be reformed. Calling a person a 'wrongdoer' is seen as likely to produce a blaming attitude, which the method seeks to avoid. Unlike restorative practice, the method does not seek to obtain an apology from the bully. The focus is upon a transformation of an individual from one who behaves hurtfully to one who is motivated through empathic feelings to give help.

The Support Group Method also differs from restorative practice in the way it makes use of selected peers of the students who are involved in the bullying. Peers are invariably present at meetings that are held with the bullies, not to assist in ensuring that 'justice is done', but rather to help to bring about support for the victim. They constitute a sort of pressure group that can influence the bullies toward acting in a pro-social and positive way in their subsequent interactions with the person they had victimized. They also provide a source of constructive ideas about how the situation can be improved.

Unlike restorative practice, there is never any involvement on the part of significant adults, as is the case in Community Conferences when parents and other adults may be present. The wider community of 'significant others' do not play a part in the Support Group Method.

Finally, the bullies and the group of peers who are convened to help resolve the problem have a shared responsibility in doing so. The practitioner plays a facilitative role rather than one that acts directly to ensure that a desired outcome is reached.

The Seven Steps

There are seven steps in the Support Group Method, beginning with an interview with the victim; then holding a meeting with a group of students including both the bullies and other students (but not the victim); and ending with meetings with the individuals who have taken part in the application of the method.

Step 1 – Talking with the victim

The practitioner meets with the victim to establish the impact that the bullying has had. The victim is not asked to describe particular incidents in which bullying has taken place, but is encouraged to provide a detailed and graphic account of the distress that he or she has experienced. This may take the form of a piece of writing or a drawing that expresses how the child has been affected by the bullying. The victim is asked to identify the 'bullies' and to suggest the names of people to form a group who could help solve the problem. Assurance is given that no one will be punished.

Step 2 – Convening a group meeting

This meeting includes the children who have been identified as those engaging in the bullying, and some other students who are selected by the practitioner because they are expected to be helpful in bringing about a positive outcome. The victim is not required to be present. Generally the size of the group is around six to eight.

Step 3 – Explaining the problem

The practitioner draws attention to the problem and especially to the distress that the victim is experiencing, using evidence provided by the victim. Specific incidents are not described and no accusations are made.

Step 4 – Promoting shared responsibility

It is made clear that no one is going to be punished and that the group has been convened to help solve the problem and that everyone has a responsibility to improve the situation.

Step 5 – Asking for ideas

The practitioner asks for suggestions about how things can be made better for the victim. Each person present is asked to make a personal statement on what he or she will do to help.

Step 6 – Leaving it up to them

Having explained the situation, the practitioner passes responsibility for the problem over to the group, thanks them for their support, and indicates that there will be further meetings with each of the students to see how things are going.

Step 7 – Final meetings

A week or so later the practitioner meets with members of the group individually to ascertain progress. The victim is also interviewed as part of the monitoring process.

It is important to recognize that, although no one is being blamed for the bullying, this approach is quite confrontative and insists that the children present have a joint responsibility to improve the situation for the victim. In extreme cases, as when there have been serious assaults, a disciplinary approach is seen as more appropriate and involves the application of sanctions and possible police action.

Critique

With many teachers the Support Group Method approach has proved to be popular. It has, however, been the target of some criticism and indeed censure. Foremost among the critics have been government leaders in England. For instance, during the 1990s then Prime Minister Blair was reported as being shocked by the widespread use of the method by local education authorities and schools. He described it as both dangerous and reckless. This attack, strongly supported by his Minister for Education, David Blunkett, was followed by a government announcement that teachers were to be given greater powers to punish pupils. The government, it seems, had to be seen as challenging and tough on bad behavior. Kidscape, a prominent and outspoken critic of the method, was particularly incensed, stating unequivocally that "bullies should apologise to victims, feel ashamed of what they've done, and there should be consequences – or they will go through life thinking they can do anything they wish to others". Dan Olweus, a strong critic of the method was cited as saying "it would be very unfortunate if schools tried to use it, instead of more effective methods".[2] As a result of such pressure, the Support Group Method was judged to be unacceptable by some anti-bullying organizations such as the influential Anti-Bullying Alliance in Britain. Nevertheless it continues to be used in many schools throughout the world.

The criticism of the Support Group Method is largely misguided. Bullying behavior in schools is on a continuum of severity, with only a small amount of bullying taking extreme forms such as serious assaults. The public at large are rightly most concerned about such incidents and alarmed at the prospect of them being treated as if they were minor misdemeanors and going unpunished. Governments tend to play upon such fears, and represent all, or practically all, bullying as being at the severe end of the bullying continuum. They choose to ignore the proviso made by the users of the Support Group Method that extreme incidents do require the use of sterner measures.

Critics also take exception to the philosophy underlying the method, which is that blaming individuals for their involvement in bullying incidents is not helpful in bringing about a successful resolution to the problem. This view is taken – by critics – to mean that the person who engages in bullying is not responsible for any reprehensible behavior. What they fail to understand is that the practitioners of this method do not absolve the participants in the bullying from any responsibility for what has happened. Rather, they view responsibility to help as something that is shared by a group of students, including the 'bullies', especially after they have been made aware of the harm that has been done. These students have a responsibility to take action to improve matters.

'Nonblaming' is seen as a means of bringing about a desirable outcome. It does not imply that the children who have engaged in the bullying are not responsible for what they have done. Unfortunately many people have not understood it this way and have engaged in much misguided criticism. The originators of this method, Barbara Maines and George Robinson, wisely took the pragmatic course of action. They changed the name from the 'No Blame Approach' to the 'Support Group Approach', but the method and its rationale remained the same.

An important assumption in this method is that the students who have bullied someone can be motivated to respond empathically to the plight of their target. This assumption is sometimes challenged. It is argued that 'bullies lack empathy'. It is possible to point to research that does in fact show that, on average, those children identified as bullies score higher than others on a measure of psychoticism[3] and on machiavellianism.[4] These findings do not, however, mean that those children who bully lack empathy, only that it is likely that in them it may be more difficult to arouse. As we have seen, the Support Group Method puts considerable emphasis upon providing evidence of the distress of targets of bullying in order to produce an emotional response.

A further assumption made by the practitioners of the method is that when bullying occurs it is commonly the case that a number of students are involved as perpetrators. Hence, in the usual application of the method, a number of students who have been identified as bullies are brought together and are viewed as having a responsibility, together with others, to act to solve the problem. The assumption of group involvement in cases of bullying is, as indicated earlier, consistent with research finding.

The method does not, however, normally allow for explorations of any justification that group members may feel for their acts of bullying (as when the victim is considered provocative). The group dynamics which have an important bearing upon how the problem is resolved are not examined, as occurs, for instance, in applying the Method of Shared Concern approach.[5] This is an important limitation of the Support Group Method.

Some questions may be raised about the more specific aspects of the method. One view is critical of seeing the victim first, that is, before the suspected bullies are seen. It is sometimes claimed that this procedure puts the victim at greater risk because he or she can be accused of getting the bullies in trouble and lead to recrimination. This is possible, and there is much to be said for convening a support group with bullies present *with minimum delay* before any mischief can be done. When it is explained at the meeting that no one is going to be punished, the risk of recrimination is much reduced. It is also worth reflecting that, in most cases, news of the bullying has already been disclosed by the victim or the victim's parents so the opportunity to meet with the bullies first is often impractical.

Whether the bullies should be seen individually or in a group is sometimes a contentious issue. Meeting them in a group rather than as individuals has some advantages. It can establish that there is a group responsibility to solve the problem. It also avoids the time-consuming task of arranging and conducting individual interviews. However, even in the presence of well-chosen pro-social students, a group of bullies can make it difficult for the practitioner, especially if they act in a defiant way and continually reinforce each other. This is more likely to happen with older students who are less amenable to influence by teachers. Establishing a constructive relationship and an empathic appreciation of the problem is generally easier to achieve in a one-to-one situation.

The practitioners of the Support Group Method claim that by convening groups of students, including perpetrators and others, and working with them, they are able to facilitate a problem-solving out-come without imposing their solutions upon anyone. This certainly contrasts with the more directive methods employed in many inter-ventions. However, having set up a situation in which a subgroup of pro-social students are likely to influence a subgroup of bullies, there is always the possibility that the bullies act positively because they have been, to some degree, coerced by the group pressure. Care must be taken in applying this method to ensure, as far as possible, that actions taken by the participants in the group meeting are what the individuals choose to do.

The method appears to make assumptions about the nature of children who are victimized by peers. Although, as we have seen, by far the majority are what may be termed 'innocent' victims, that is, children who have in no way provoked the bullying, this is not always so. Sometimes victims are provocative. This does not mean, of course, that they do not deserve to be helped. But it does make the reservations some bullies have about helping to improve the situation for the victim understandable. It is far from clear how the Support Group Method handles this situation, as the focus is almost exclusively on the plight of the victim. The understandable reservations some students may have in improving the victim's situation do need to be addressed, as they are, for instance, in the Method of Shared Concern.

Another assumption sometimes made is that the victim is doing all that is possible to prevent being bullied. Hence, efforts to increase the power of the victim to resist are seen as futile. While in many cases this is certainly the case – as when there is a big and unbridgeable imbalance of power – strengthening the victim can sometimes be a realistic option.

It has been suggested that the Support Group Method may not be supported by parents. This is likely to be true of some parents, especially the parents of children who have been victimized and feel very angry about it. They may well feel that a punitive response is needed from the school. A school may therefore be challenged to justify its approach. It needs to be explained to parents that the method has a high prospect of success in preventing their child from being bullied again, and this may be for them a higher priority than seeing that the perpetrator is punished. In communities where a vengeful approach is particularly strong, meetings with parents to explain how, why, and when the Support Group Approach is being used is needed.

Unlike some applications of restorative practice, such as community conferences, the method does not take into account wider ramifications of bullying. It does not recognize that there are other relevant influences on a child's behavior that need to be taken into account besides the child's peers. There are often adults who play a significant part in a child's life and their influence can be harnessed in Community Conferences.[6]

How does the Support Group Method measure up to other methods of interventions? Some authorities have derided the method and reported (without any data) that it is ineffective. However, a number of studies have provided results that suggest that it is often effective in preventing bullying from continuing.

Some of the evaluations have been carried out by practitioners of the method. A study in England of 55 cases in which the method was used (with minor modifications) reported in 1998 that:

> The approach has been successful in the great majority of cases – to be precise the bullying stopped completely or the victim no longer felt in need of support.[7]

In a further study of 12 cases in which the method was used, it was reported that 11 of them had been dealt with successfully.[8]

As is the case with most evaluations, reports from *nonpractitioners* of the method are rare. An exception is a report contained in a study led by a distinguished English academic in 2007.[9] Ratings of the effectiveness of the method were obtained from 59 schools in England where the method had been employed. The average rating from teachers, parents, and students was 'very satisfactory'. Further research is needed, especially research conducted by researchers who can take a more neutral or objective stance so as to avoid the possibility of bias in reporting. However, there is currently sufficient evidence supporting the method for it to be taken seriously as a useful method of intervention in cases of nonsevere bullying.

The Future

The sustained and unfair criticism of the Support Group Method, motivated largely it seems by political considerations, has made it difficult for the method to be judged objectively. As long as the focus is on extreme forms of violence and the fears that the general population have about children being criminally assaulted, progress in the adoption of the method will be slow and uncertain. Fortunately, many teachers, especially in England, strongly support the Support Group Method and find it useful – and acceptable – as a way of dealing with cases of bullying.

Endnotes

1   Barbara Maines and George Robinson (see Robinson & Maines, 1997) are the originators of this highly influential approach, originally called the No Blame Approach; they later changed the name to the Support Group Method.

2   See observations on the No Blame Approach on the Kidscape website at http://www.kidscape.org.uk/press/131200NoBlameReasons.shtml

3 Two Australian researchers, Rigby and Slee (1993), have demonstrated a low but statistically significant relationship between a measure of psychoticism as assessed on the Eysenck Personality Inventory and self-reports of bullying others. This suggests that children who bully tend to be relatively indifferent to the pain they inflict.

4 In the UK, Sutton and Keogh (2001) have noted that bullies tend to be somewhat machiavellian in how they treat others; that is, they are more likely than others to manipulate situations in their own interest.

5 See Chapter 9 for an account of the Method of Shared Concern.

6 See Chapter 7 for a description of Community Conferences as a restorative practice.

7 Sue Young (1998) evaluated a modified version of the No Blame Approach devised by Maines and Robinson.

8 This further evaluation of the Support Group Method was undertaken by Young and Haldorf (2003).

9 Smith *et al.* (2007) surveyed schools and local education authorities to obtain information on the use of the method and outcomes from its use.

Chapter 9

The Method of Shared Concern

The Method of Shared Concern is the most comprehensive and complex method for addressing cases of bullying so far considered in this book. Arguably, it needs to be complex because bullying is itself a complex phenomenon and needs to be responded to at different levels.

This method originated through the work of a Swedish psychologist, Anatol Pikas.[1] The name he gave to the Method was 'Shared Concern Method', abbreviated as SCm. Some have continued to use this title. However, most writers have used a more anglicized nomenclature and called it 'The Method of Shared Concern'.[2]

It is in some ways akin to both the Support Group Method and the mediation approach, but different in important respects from both. Like the Support Group Method, it adopts a nonblaming approach in working with the students who are involved in the problem. Like the mediation approach, it recognizes that students in conflict with each other may be helped through mediation. They may not be willing – or able – to arrive at a mutually acceptable resolution without assistance from the practitioner.

Bullying Interventions in Schools: Six Basic Approaches, First Edition. Ken Rigby.
© 2012 Ken Rigby. Published 2012 by Blackwell Publishing Ltd.

A crucial distinguishing feature of the Method of Shared Concern is the requirement that the practitioner work on the problem with the suspected bullies first as individuals, and then in a group. This strategy is a radical departure from what generally happens in the application of some other methods; for instance, in the Support Group Method the suspected bullies are first seen in a group.

Bullying is often viewed as located in the personality and motivations of the individual student, who is conceived as aberrant, uncivilized, or even evil. The social context in which the individual operates is virtually ignored or discounted. The aim becomes one of changing that person by one means or another, through the use of threats and punishment, re-integrative shaming, or through the eliciting of empathic feelings. The Method of Shared Concern recognizes a dimension that is often ignored, that is, the connectedness or interdependence that exists between students involved in bullying someone. Hence, in any attempt to deal effectively with a case of bullying there needs to be induced a positive change in how the group functions and how its operation affects the individual members.

This approach also recognizes that in cases of bullying there is sometimes a degree of provocation on the part of the victim. It is thought that when this occurs, it is important to include in the application of the method a systematic mediational process.

The Application of the Method of Shared Concern

Pikas, the originator of the Shared Concern Method, has provided no manual or writings in English describing in detail how the method should be applied. His influence in Australia has been largely through workshops he conducted in 1994 and 2006 which I attended. There have been variations in interpretation and application of the method. For instance, one description provided by the Australian *Friendly Schools and Families* initiative includes only the first two stages of the procedure.[3]

In 2007, a DVD was produced by Readymade Productions to provide training for teachers in the use of what was described as the

Method of Shared Concern.[4] The following describes how the method is understood by the present writer.

First, individuals involved in a bully/victim problem are identified. Reliable information is needed in relation to

- the person or persons being bullied by another individual or group, and
- the person or persons continually engaged in carrying out the bullying.

Ideally this information is obtained through observations, for example, by teachers, and/or by receiving reports, as distinct from talking directly with the person being targeted. Sometimes, however, the child or parent may report the incident to a staff member. In such cases, a child may be at risk for allegedly informing on the bullies, and care needs to be taken to ensure the child's protection. The risk is reduced when it is explained to all concerned that no punishment is intended.

Next, a number of students are identified as likely to have taken part in the bullying, or to have supported it in some way. These students are regarded as 'suspected bullies', that is, students who may or may not have engaged in the bullying. At no stage are steps taken to establish blame and to convict anyone. Each student is seen in turn, starting (if known) with the likely ringleader. Under some circumstances, if desired, other students aware of the problem – for example, bystanders – may be included, as they may play an important role in influencing the bullying.

Each interview must take place in private and without interruption. The meeting begins with the interviewer inviting the student to sit down opposite without an intervening desk. The interviewer waits for eye contact before the interaction begins. At these meetings with individual students it is important not to make any accusations.

Practitioners first explain their role – to help children feel safe at school. They then point out that it has been noticed that a particular student (who is named) is having a hard time at school with other students. The practitioner then describes what is known about the plight of this student, for example, his being upset, isolated or staying away from school. Once the concerns of the practitioner have been clearly – and sincerely – conveyed, the student is asked to say what he or she has noticed or knows about that person's situation. (Typically the suspected bully acknowledges the person's distress, but is not asked what part he or she might have played.)

As soon as the student has acknowledged some awareness (not guilt, nor remorse) about what has been happening, they are asked directly what can be done to help improve matters. The practitioner is not trying to 'get to the bottom of the matter' and apportion blame, but to produce a constructive response that will help to change the situation.

Commonly, the student does make suggestions about what can be done. But if not, the practitioner may make suggestions – ones that are not difficult to carry out. Strong approval is expressed for any constructive proposals made (or agreed to) by the suspected bully. Another meeting (at an agreed time) is arranged; the aim of this meeting will be to see how things have gone. Importantly, at no stage at this first meeting are any threats made or any warnings given. The remaining students identified as suspected bullies or bystanders are seen individually and the procedure repeated.

After all of the suspected bullies have been seen, the targeted person is interviewed. Practitioners begin by explaining their role and asking how things are going, expressing concern, sympathy, and support over what has been happening. It is important that a trusting relationship is developed. However, questions need to be asked to find out whether the target has been doing something to bring on the bullying – that is, by acting as a provocative victim. Importantly, no blame should be directed at the student. This line of questioning must be done sensitively. Commonly the victim is innocent. The practitioner then discloses that he or she has already talked individually with a number of students involved in the bullying and there has been an undertaking on their part to do things to improve the situation. The target is asked to look out for signs of change in the behavior of the bullies. Arrangements are made to meet again to monitor progress.

Several days later, follow-up meetings are held with individual bullies (as previously arranged). The aim here is to ascertain whether the suspected bullies have carried out actions, as they have promised, to improve the situation. Only when the practitioner is satisfied that progress is being made can a meeting be convened with the whole group of suspected bullies.

At the ensuing group meeting (without the victim being present), the group is congratulated for having taken steps to improve the situation, and each member may be asked to describe what he or she has done to try to improve the situation. It then becomes possible to prepare the group for the next stage: a meeting to which the victim will be invited. If the members of the group are now ready to act unreservedly in a positive and friendly manner toward the person they had targeted, the final or summit meeting can be expected to result in a cessation of the bullying and in the establishment of good relations.

However, the practitioner should bear in mind that sometimes the group members may believe that the target has been, in some ways, provocative or unreasonable, and concessions or adjustments may be required. Discussion is needed to consider any reservations that the group or members of the group may have about how they are to relate to the target. The practitioner may help them formulate a proposal to put to the target but, importantly, the members of the group need to 'own' any proposed solution to the conflict. Before the end of the meeting, each member of the group and/or a spokesperson for the group is asked to indicate what they are prepared to say at the final meeting. Such thorough preparation of the group for this meeting is essential.

At a subsequent brief meeting between the practitioner and the target, he or she can normally be induced to join the group for a final meeting, with assurances that progress can be made at the meeting. However, if the target is not willing to come along, his or her feelings and decision must be respected.

At the summit meeting with the suspected bullies and the target all present, the students are enabled by the practitioner to express their thoughts about how they wish to proceed to resolve the issue. Typically, the suspected bullies will have, in fact, experienced a sense of genuine concern about the target's plight and already have taken steps to improve relations. The meeting then serves the purpose of establishing that the problem has been successfully addressed – essentially by the students themselves.

There are some occasions when each side harbors resentment and is not ready to call a closure to the problem. This can occur when the target has behaved provocatively and the 'bullies' want to see a change in the target's behavior before they will change. In such circumstances, the suspected bullies may require that the victim changes his or her behavior before they are prepared to change theirs. At the summit meeting, they make a proposal to that effect, one formulated with the practitioner's help during the previous group meeting. (Some preparation may also have been carried out earlier with the targeted person, so that he or she may be ready to make any necessary concessions.) At this stage, the practitioner plays the role of the neutral mediator. Typically, adjustments take place on each side. The aim here is to help the students reach an acceptable agreement about how each will behave toward the other in future. This may (if deemed necessary) take the form of a written contract which everyone signs. Finally, the practitioner is expected to discuss with the students what they might do if they relapse and the problem recurs – and to emphasize the need to keep channels of communication open.

Critique

The Method of Shared Concern is the most ambitious of all the methods so far designed to address cases of bullying in schools. It seeks to combine an understanding of the psychology of individual students who have taken part in bullying with an understanding of relevant group processes. It recognizes that not all cases of bullying are alike and incorporates a procedure that is especially relevant when the targeted student has acted provocatively and a mediation approach becomes necessary.

Pikas, the originator of the Shared Concern Method, saw the approach as basically therapeutic. He was interested not only in stopping the bullying but in restoring the health or well-being of those who had participated. Good mental health was seen as consisting in being able to act constructively and also autonomously, that is, not driven to act in a way determined by a peer group or friendship group or by authority figures.

In evaluating the method, it is useful to consider the assumptions that are made in attempting this task:

1. Bullying in schools is typically, if not always, undertaken primarily by individuals under the influence of a number of peers with whom they commonly associate. In this respect, it is similar to the Support Group Method and is well supported by research.
2. Also as in the case of the Support Group Method, considerable trust is placed in the capacity of the 'bullies' to respond empathically. (This trust may occasionally be misplaced with respect to a minority of students.)
3. It is best to first meet with those students who are suspected of bullying individually, rather than in a group. The justification for this view is partly pragmatic. Students who have been bullying as a group or under the influence of a group are likely to be much more resistant, and supportive of each other's resistance, when they are encountered as a group by someone who is perceived as seeking to change their behavior. This is even more likely to be the case when the 'someone' is an authority figure.
4. This approach is more appropriately applied with adolescent students. In part, this is because they are much less likely to be influenced by authoritative suggestions from teachers. Typically they become more critical and nonaccepting of the influence of institutional authority figures.[5] Arguably too, older students are more able to appreciate the nature of the group dynamics which influence their behavior. It has nevertheless been claimed that the Method of Shared Concern has been used effectively with preadolescent children.[6]
5. Meeting with the suspected bullies individually provides an opportunity for the development of a trusting relationship between the practitioner and each student, especially if the practitioner behaves in a nonjudgmental way and concentrates on understanding the situation from the student's point of view. This enables the practitioner to influence each student's attitudes and behavior more readily. However, as indicated earlier, it has been suggested that in moving toward a kind of therapist–client

relationship, the practitioner may be minimizing the role of the group as the prime problem-solvers. Occasionally students may think that the practitioner is unable to improve the situation and, if there is recrimination for 'telling', the situation may get worse. There are reported cases of victims declining an invitation to meet with the bullies in the summit meeting because they still fear the bullies or wish to avoid embarrassment. Although these cases appear to be rare, difficulties may arise with some victims when their involvement is sought, and the development of a trusting relationship with the victim is of great importance.

6. Once progress has been made with individual bullies and actual steps have been taken by them to improve the situation for the victim, there are grounds for expecting that their attitudes toward the victim will have improved also. This belief is consistent with the well-supported theory of cognitive dissonance which asserts that attitude-change typically follows any behavioral change that is induced, especially if it is not forced.[7] Evidence of behavior change provides a good basis for expecting subsequent group meetings to have positive outcomes.

7. Further changes in the attitudes and behavior of individuals are likely to come about in the course of interacting as part of the group convened by the practitioner. In many cases changes will already have begun due to (i) having felt some concern for the target during the individual interview and (ii) having undertaken some action to help improve the situation. In the group context they learn that other students are thinking along the same lines. They may come to realize that their private thoughts and feelings are not different from those of others; that is, they no longer are handicapped in their behavior by what has been termed 'pluralistic ignorance'.[8] They are exposed to the real feelings of others about the victim, which may be quite different from what they imagined. Subtly the dynamics of the group begin to change. In some cases, the ringleader may lose the power to influence the others.

8. The group remains an important influence on the behavior of the individual members. It is not assumed that the group becomes irrelevant to its members. Hopefully, they are now individually

more autonomous. But the agreement among themselves that they will behave differently toward the victim will have a continuing influence.

9. Finally in the application of the Method of Shared Concern, the group meetings are seen as vital. They have an important educational function and are extremely helpful in ensuring a sustainable solution (unfortunately some educators recommend omitting the group meeting stage).

In general, the assumptions made in the Method of Shared Concern are well supported, but there are several practical difficulties that have concerned some educators. The first relates to the practicality of seeing the victim only after the bullies have been seen individually. In practice this is rarely possible, as the victim, or the victim's parents, will have been in contact with the school to complain. The danger that this presents to the victim can be minimized by making it clear to the bullies that there is no intention of applying any form of punishment.

The second difficulty is that the process can be time-consuming and difficult for poorly resourced schools to undertake. As noted above, some educators have suggested a truncated version – without the group meetings of the practitioner, victim, and suspected bullies – as a possible solution. This option could be considered in cases in which there is a strong acceptance of responsibility on the part of all the suspected bullies to help the victim, and actions are undertaken to improve the situation. But there are dangers in following this course. When students meet again in a group without the presence of the practitioner, they may revert to their earlier bullying behavior. Working through the issue in a practitioner-led group, especially when there are signs that not all members are happy with the emerging situation, can give the school greater confidence that the problem has been resolved.

Thirdly, a difficulty may arise because the method is more complex than others and practitioners do need to receive training in its use. However, there are a growing number of useful resources which can help some teachers to develop the necessary understanding of the method and acquire the relevant skills.

The Method of Shared Concern has been evaluated in several studies. In a small-scale study conducted in secondary schools in Sheffield, England, reductions in bullying were reported for three out of four students on whom the method was applied. Five of the six teachers responsible for employing the approach claimed that it had reduced the frequency and severity of the bullying.[9] A study in Scotland reported that the approach was applied successfully or very successfully in 34 out of 38 cases among children aged between 7 and 16 years.[10] In Western Australia, a success rate of over 85 percent has been claimed following the application of the approach by school personnel/school psychologists in upper primary and lower secondary school.[11] In general, the approach has been highly rated by its users. In a survey of 155 schools across England, an average rating for the Method of Shared Concern was 3.9 – this was on a 5-point scale where 1 equaled not at all satisfied and 5 was extremely satisfied.[12] Finally, in a report provided to the Australian Federal Department of Education, Employment and Workplace Relations (DEEWR), it was claimed that in applications of the approach at 17 schools in Australia, positive outcomes were found in 15 cases that were addressed by teachers and counselors.[13] This report was in some respects an advance on previous evaluations of the Method of Shared Concern, in that post-application interviews with the participants were not undertaken by the practitioner but by another member of staff, thereby minimizing experimenter bias.

There is then considerable evidence suggesting that the Method of Shared Concern can be effective in addressing a large proportion of cases. At the same time, it is evident that ratings of success provided by practitioners could contain some possibly unconscious bias in favor of the method.

The Future

The future of the Method of Shared Concern, as with the Support Group Method and to a lesser degree restorative practices, depends on the extent to which the traditional disciplinary approach retains its popularity. It is highly unlikely that the Method of Shared Concern will replace all the others. But it may well make headway under the following conditions:

- If the traditional disciplinary approach loses favor in areas in which alternative approaches are more acceptable – that is, in relation to cases that are not so severe.
- In cases in which it is deemed unreasonable to expect the 'bully' to feel and express remorse, and the negative consequences of applying undue pressure to bring about a sense of shame could lead to stigmatization.
- In cases in which the bullying is to some extent elicited and sustained by resentment felt toward the 'provocative' victim. It is in this area that the Method of Shared Concern may be viewed as superior to the Support Group Method.
- In circumstances in which there are well-trained practitioners who are able to use the method effectively. It is probably fair to say that the Method of Shared Concern puts more demands upon the practitioner than any other method.

Endnotes

1   Anatol Pikas, a Swedish psychologist, initiated and has been developing the Shared Concern Method for over 20 years. Published accounts of the approach can be found in Pikas (1989, 2002).
2   See Smith *et al.* (2004b), Sullivan (2000), Lewers and Murphy (2000), Rigby (2005b), and McGrath and Noble (2006).
3   See Erceg and Cross (2004).
4   This DVD was made for Readymade Productions by Christopher Faul, supported by a grant from the Australian Federal Department of Education, Employment and Workplace Relations (DEEWR). It provides an enactment by students and two practitioners of a version of the Method of Shared Concern as interpreted by Ken Rigby. See Readymade Productions (2007).
5   See Rigby *et al.* (1987).

6   See Duncan (1996).
7   The highly influential theory of cognitive dissonance was proposed by Leon Festinger (1957).
8   It has been long recognized that people commonly misperceive how other people think and feel about events, typically by seeing people as less altruistic or thoughtful than they are. See Allport (1924).
9   Reported in Smith and Sharp (1994) in describing research undertaken in the Sheffield Project.
10 See Duncan (1996).
11 See Griffiths (2001).
12 See Smith (2001).
13 This report, funded by the Department of Education, Employment and Workplace Relations (DEEWR), was undertaken in South Australia, Victoria, Tasmania, and Western Australia, by Rigby and Griffiths (2010). It was released in January 2010, and can be accessed through www.deewr.gov.au/schooling/nationalsafeschools/pages/research. aspx.

Part 3

The Choice of Intervention Method

Having examined each of the six selected intervention strategies, the obvious question is: which is the best? A reasonable question perhaps, but on reflection not one that can be unequivocally or even reasonably answered. There are so many things to be considered before any of the six approaches can be used in preference to others. A better question is: under what circumstances might it be best to use one approach rather than another? That is the question I will try to answer in this part of the book.

Some of the answers will be influenced, if not determined, by broad considerations that are inseparable from how the school operates as a whole. These are matters to be considered in Chapter 10: the social philosophy of the school, knowledge and understanding that exists in the school on how cases of bullying can be addressed, acceptance by the school and the community of the use of particular methods, and finally the availability of resources needed for the employment of each method. All these factors must be considered before a school decides what action it might take in particular cases of bullying.

Bullying Interventions in Schools: Six Basic Approaches, First Edition. Ken Rigby.
© 2012 Ken Rigby. Published 2012 by Blackwell Publishing Ltd.

We can then turn to the next question to be explored in Chapter 11 which is: what method is it best to use in particular cases? This involves a further examination of the six methods, this time to suggest when particular methods may be most applicable and what factors may determine the choices schools and individual teachers make.

Finally, we return in Chapter 12 to the main thesis of the book and reflect upon the current situation.

Chapter 10

The School and the Community

The Social Philosophy of the School

Every school has a social philosophy, implicit or explicit, that provides a view to how children who behave badly are to be treated. By 'social philosophy' I mean the values, attitudes, and assumptions that are held by members of the school community, which guide the way members of a school community are expected to relate to each other. This philosophy helps to determine how the school will handle cases of bullying.

Often the social philosophy of a school is embedded in tradition. Staff may say: "This is the way we deal with bullies at this school – always have. It's *our* way". Generally speaking, the longer the tradition the more likely it will stress 'obedience' and 'discipline'. Schools with this philosophy will naturally be drawn toward the traditional disciplinary approach. There are, of course, other traditions, such as one that favors a more democratic approach to problem-solving. This philosophy may lead to the encouragement of student participation in solving interpersonal problems, rather than having solutions

Bullying Interventions in Schools: Six Basic Approaches, First Edition. Ken Rigby.
© 2012 Ken Rigby. Published 2012 by Blackwell Publishing Ltd.

imposed upon them. A tradition may have its roots in religious beliefs about how people ought to be treated; for instance, there may be a tradition supported by religious belief that says that children who express sincere remorse at having bullied someone should not be punished – instead, they will be forgiven.

This is not to suggest that the school community is entirely at one in its acceptance of a given philosophy, or that the nature of the prevailing philosophy cannot change. Over time, it may evolve or change, sometimes quite quickly.

A case in point concerns a non-state school with a long and venerable history in Australia, to which I was invited in the 1990s. The invitation came from a newly appointed principal who had become exceedingly alarmed at a serious problem of bullying that had come to light at his school, and had also agitated and angered many parents. Worse still, lurid accounts of bullying by senior boys in the dormitories of the boarding school had made their way to the press. After speaking with staff members, it became evident to me that the bullying was being supported or sustained by a philosophy that reflected a nineteenth-century view of student management. I was irresistibly reminded of *Tom Brown's Schooldays*. Senior boys were encouraged to keep order by subduing the younger boys by any means they saw fit. Adult supervision of the dormitories was slack. It was said that the staff turned a blind eye to what was going on. Even some of the younger boys justified what was happening on the grounds that "it will be our turn when we are seniors". Meanwhile the younger students absorbed the pain and humiliation – and waited for their junior years to pass. Some staff members believed that their school 'toughened them up'. Some parents, too. Consistent with the pride the school felt in their reputation as champions at rugby, it was reported that the younger children were selected to be 'tackling bags'.

With the advent of a new principal the situation changed quickly. This was made possible by two factors. One was the pressure brought to bear on the school by the media and meetings with parents. The other involved a series of meetings with teachers and parents that I conducted and at which alternative ways of addressing problems of bullying were discussed. The changes that followed were helpful. The level of bullying was assessed using a reliable questionnaire at the time of my inquiry, and a year later the bullying had reduced considerably. This could reasonably be attributed to a change in social philosophy from an antiquated nineteenth-century philosophy on how to manage schoolboys to a more enlightened late twentieth-century attitude.

Knowledge and Understanding of the Methods Available to Address Cases of School Bullying

Readers who have come thus far in this book will not be surprised to hear that the average teacher's knowledge and understanding of what can be done to address cases of bullying is often severely limited. This must be extended if new approaches are to be considered and implemented. It is not enough to have an enlightened philosophy. The practitioner must also have the requisite technical knowledge of methods of intervention, and an understanding of their rationale.[1]

Sometimes a teacher or counselor has a smattering of knowledge about a particular method and assumes that he or she has a realistic grasp of what is entailed. A word or catchphrase relating to the method has passed their way, and a misguided impression has been formed. A somewhat farcical instance of confusion over the Method of Shared Concern occurred at a workshop I ran. Prior to explaining this approach, I asked whether anyone present had actually practiced it. One teacher earnestly explained that the method was being used at her school and was proving to be effective. Much encouraged, I asked her to say how it was being applied. She replied that everyone at her school was now going around saying how concerned they were about students who were being bullied. At another workshop I was told by a teacher that his school had improved the way the Method of Shared Concern was applied. He explained that after a student had indicated what he or she would do to improve a situation and was about to leave the room, the practitioner would fire a parting shot: "Hey, you know what will happen if you don't!" – thereby revealing to the workshop members that he had no understanding at all of the philosophy underlying the method.

Most misunderstandings are perhaps not so egregious or hilarious. But anyone who has listened to descriptions of particular methods of intervention as they are implemented at a school will recognize that there is a remarkable degree of confusion about what the methods entail. Procedures that form part of one approach are combined with procedures that on rational grounds are incompatible with the thinking underlying another. For instance, one cannot reasonably combine a nonblaming approach with one that contains punitive elements. Methods that depend largely on the eliciting of empathy for a victim are different from methods that are designed to produce shame – however reintegratively – or remorse. You cannot reasonably insist that a child must make an apology and expect the child to do so sincerely.

This is not to say that a mix and match approach is always impossible, or that a practitioner may not begin with a method of intervention according to 'the book' and adapt it to be in accord with how she can personally operate best. The psychologist, Sidney Jourard, a trainer of psychotherapists, once declared that he would only give a stamp of approval – a gold star – to his trainees when they were able to demonstrate their mastery of a counseling method by applying it precisely according to the technical requirements that had been laid down. He then added that if after a year or so the trainee was still doing exactly the same, he would take the gold star away.[2] But first the methods and their rationale must be understood.

Acceptance by the school and the community of the actual use of particular methods

Intervening in ways that are contrary to procedures approved by the school is likely to be counterproductive, however justified the practitioner may believe the intervention to be. What is acceptable to the school will in part be determined by what I have called the school philosophy, but also in part by the knowledge and understanding that members of the school community have of the available methods. In some schools, the acceptable method or methods may be prescribed in the school anti-bullying policy. The teachers and counselors may have little or no choice in how they treat cases of bullying. In other schools, there may be some uncertainty about what approaches are acceptable and clarification will be needed. Fruitful debate may ensue and new and better ways of dealing with cases may be discovered.

One obvious implication is that each member of staff needs to be well acquainted with the alternatives or options open to the school. But bear in mind that the approach or approaches chosen may need to be acceptable to the wider community, especially to the parents of the students. It is unlikely that a consensus can be achieved among parents: some are likely to favor a strong disciplinary approach and others a more nonpunitive approach. On pragmatic grounds attention must be paid to what parents think, but the starting point in my view is what is thought by the staff and, especially, by the leadership in a school. Moreover, the school has an educational role that extends beyond the school, and can help the community to appraise alternative approaches more objectively and reflect upon them. Recently, at one Australian primary school I visited, parents were invited to discuss with the staff the six methods of intervention presented in this book.

Endnotes

1   Since I began to write this book, I have become aware of a very recent publication which describes a range of nonpunitive methods of intervention in cases of bullying. This short book provides very useful, practical information for teachers who are interested in the application of alternative methods (see Renn *et al.* 2009). In addition, there is now available a DVD that I helped to make in England in 2009 called: 'Bullying in Schools: Six Methods of Intervention', produced by Loggerhead Films. See www.prlog. org/10398874-bullying-in-schools-6-methods-of-intervention.html. This DVD comprises practical demonstration of the approaches outlined in this book.

2   A pearl of wisdom from a leading humanistic psychologist of the 1960s, Sidney M. Jourard (1964).

Chapter 11

Choosing a Method

Let us assume first that the school is prepared to support each one of the six methods of intervention and has the resources to implement them. I know that this may be a tall order at some schools, but bear with me. Given this ideal state, what criteria should guide a school in choosing one or more methods when intervening in a particular case of bullying?

We can begin by making a brief summary of the six methods, the assumptions they make, and what conclusions can reasonably be made about their use.

The Traditional Disciplinary Approach

The traditional disciplinary approach makes the assumption that bullying is best controlled through the use of negative consequences – penalties, sanctions, punishments. These deter the bully from continuing to bully and also others who see what has happened to the bully. Moreover justice is achieved for the victim.

Bullying Interventions in Schools: Six Basic Approaches, First Edition. Ken Rigby.
© 2012 Ken Rigby. Published 2012 by Blackwell Publishing Ltd.

Sounds reasonable. But, as we have seen, the evidence is against this approach being used on every occasion. It was noted that around 75 percent of school authorities believe in its use even in relatively mild cases – and in many cases it simply does not succeed in stopping the bullying. This is largely because those who bully can continue to bully in ways that are difficult if not impossible to detect and, importantly, they often continue to be positively reinforced with approval from their supporters.

So when can the traditional disciplinary method best be applied? My brief answer is: not often. But a case can be made out for its use under these conditions:

1. The bullying constitutes a crime and there are legal obligations to apply sanctions.
2. There is adequate monitoring of the outcome. If the method is used frequently, surveillance of a relatively large number of 'cases' is very difficult.
3. It is used sparingly, employing light sanctions with younger children for whom teacher authority is generally more imposing and acceptable. Once again, careful monitoring is needed.
4. It is rule-driven rather than arbitrary – and the rules are justified by appealing to their general acceptance by the school community.
5. In all applications, the focus is on the inappropriateness of the behavior and not on the unworthiness of the individual, and complemented by the use of positive reinforcement of desired behavior wherever possible.

Strengthening the Victim

It is assumed that victims can be strengthened so that they can solve the problem of bullying themselves. And this can be achieved through the teaching of better social skills – especially assertiveness.

This approach is in some ways very attractive, because, if successful, it can result in greatly improved self-esteem on the part of the ex-victim and dispenses with the need for teachers to undertake interventions with dubious likelihood of success. But in many cases strengthening the victim is not a viable option. The odds confronting the victim may be too great to be overcome for the victim to have a realistic chance.

The conditions under which this approach can be successful are limited, but include the following:

1. The existence of a relatively small imbalance of power between the perpetrator(s) and the victim
2. The bullying being verbal rather than physical
3. The victim being capable of acquiring skills, both verbal and non-verbal, that are relevant to preventing the bully or bullies from continuing
4. A practitioner who is able to help the victim to develop appropriate skills, especially those of 'fogging'
5. A careful monitoring of the situation to ensure that the resistance of the victim does not result in a continuing struggle for dominance, for example, through fighting

Mediation

This approach assumes that bullies and victims can be helped to resolve their differences by working with a trained mediator, and that teachers and/or selected students can carry out this role. When it is successful, it may produce a positive and enduring outcome and bring about a more harmonious school ethos.

However, there are notable limitations on the use of this method. In some cases the parties in conflict actively resist mediation. The perpetrator may have much to lose and little to gain from reaching a peaceable solution. The teacher may find it difficult or impossible to remain neutral in addressing the problem, a prerequisite of successful mediation. Hence, situations where mediation can be undertaken in cases of bullying are relatively few. They may be identified as follows:

1. Ones in which both parties are ready to work toward a mutually acceptable solution. This is more likely when there is little imbalance of power and both parties are unhappy with the conflict continuing.
2. The teacher or counselor can reasonably remain neutral, even when the bully is manifestly abusing his or her power. (This is not to say that the practitioner should remain neutral under these conditions!)

Restorative Practices

Restorative practices assume that bullies feel remorse or can be induced to feel remorse, act restoratively, and become accepted and reintegrated into the company of those they have offended. Practices have been developed to bring this about.

The claim that all bullies feel remorse or can readily be induced to feel remorse by restorative practices may be regarded as excessive. However, some do feel remorse or can be induced, without unreasonable pressure, to feel remorse. Unless one is wedded to the idea that bullies must be made to suffer and only punishment deters, restorative practices provide an attractive option under these conditions:

1. There is evidence that the person who has bullied does feel generally remorseful or becomes remorseful after being influenced to reflect on what harm has been done.
2. The level of bullying is either not extreme or – if extreme – the use of a Community Conference is an acceptable alternative to taking legal action.
3. There are grounds for believing that an apology or restorative action will lead to the 'wrongdoer' becoming acceptable to those who have been offended. The community is forgiving and accepting.

The Support Group Method

It is assumed that when bullies recognize the harm they have caused, they are likely to want to fix it. This is seen as more likely to occur if they are not blamed and, moreover, are encouraged to act positively by other students who want the victimized child to be helped. A viable procedure can be designed to make this possible. This involves first a meeting with the victim – to gather information about the hurt – then a meeting with the bullies and some other helpful students to resolve the problem.

There are some conditions that make the Support Group Method more likely to succeed. These include the following:

1. A readiness of the perpetrators of the bullying to respond empathically to evidence provided by the practitioner of the distress experienced by the victim.
2. The availability of other students who are sympathetic toward the victim's plight to attend the meeting.
3. The Support Group Method is not applied to cases in which extreme violence has occurred and that call for a strong disciplinary approach.

The Method of Shared Concern

The basic assumption of the Method of Shared Concern is that cases of bullying are best addressed by engaging with the *groups* of students who have been involved in the bullying as well as with each of the group members individually. By meeting first with the suspected bullies as individuals, it is possible to induce each of them to acknowledge the plight of the victim, and then to act in ways that can help to improve the situation. Finally, it is assumed that subsequent group meetings with those involved can resolve the problem, if necessary involving a mediation approach.

The conditions in which the Method of Shared Concern approach is considered more appropriate are as follows:

1. A group of students have been identified as bullying a targeted individual or supporting the bullying.
2. The bullying is not of a severity that would justify punitive or legal action.
3. Students are amenable to taking part in the series of meetings that are required in order to implement the method.

4. A level of maturity exists on the part of the participants. This is normally found among most students in upper primary and secondary school.
5. The school is prepared to call upon the services of individuals trained in using the method and to allocate adequate time for its application.

This review of methods, their assumptions, and limitations will hopefully provide some ideas or suggestions about what approach to use in given situations. It will not please those who feel that there is just one best method or that one must treat all cases of bullying *in precisely the same way*. In the interest of simplification and consistency, this may be preferred by some teachers. But I am irresistibly reminded of the aphorism:

A foolish consistency is the hobgoblin of little minds.[1]

Mixed methods

Some schools develop approaches that include elements that are found in two or more of the major methods described in this book. For instance, a disciplinary approach may be used with the bully and efforts also made to strengthen the victim to withstand any future mistreatment. A restorative practice approach may be supplemented by sessions in which mediation is used to resolve any lingering resentments. An application of the Method of Shared Concern may be followed by some assertiveness training or instruction on 'fogging' to help the victim to be less vulnerable.

Incompatibilities

Yet there are some methods that cannot reasonably be combined. One cannot for instance practice a 'no blame' kind of approach when one is using a traditional disciplinary approach. One cannot view the 'bully' as a wrongdoer who *must* atone (as in restorative practice) and claim that one is leaving it to this student to act in a helpful manner after a degree of empathy for the victim has been raised (as in the Support

Group Method). The neutral stance taken by the practitioner using a mediation approach is out of place when one is applying a restorative practice approach. One cannot justify punishing a student who has failed to carry out a promise made in a Shared Concern meeting and then claim that one is using the Method of Shared Concern. This is why it is so important to understand both the techniques of intervention and the assumptions and rationale of particular methods.

Cyber Bullying

Cyber bullying is sometimes seen as adding a new dimension to school bullying and requiring a unique approach to dealing with cases. This is insofar as technical knowledge of the capabilities of electronic communication is concerned. Knowing how to block incoming messages from sources that are sending unwelcome messages can help to protect a potential victim. But technical answers are not the only consideration and arguably not the most important. Knowing what is going on *behind* the computer can take us to the core of the problem, that is, to the human relationships that have gone wrong and need mending.

As in traditional forms of bullying, cyber bullying may involve widely different levels of severity. Low-level teasing or taunting may be experienced as annoying but not intolerable. Life-threatening messages inevitably cause acute distress. Having embarrassing or offensive material about oneself posted on well-frequented sites for countless people to see can be traumatizing. In fact, some suicides are believed to have been induced by such exposure. Again, an occasional unpleasant message can be shrugged off; a continual stream of such messages is much harder to take. Where it is known or suspected that offensive messages are coming from diverse sources or with the connivance of a hostile group of people, the impact is likely to be more serious than if there is only one sender.

The receiver of abusive messages may be tempted to reply in kind, in which case the problem is likely to escalate. Alternatively, the receiver may decide to ignore and delete any offensive messages. This is sometimes a reasonable strategy. The cyber bully may be hoping for a 'desperate' reply from an injured party and, not receiving any reply, becomes discouraged. However, the requisite patience or stoicism to endure a series of insulting communications may be beyond the unfortunate victim – and help may be needed.

As many have observed, the persons targeted may not want to admit to being harmed – may in fact feel that in doing so they may be deprived of their marvelous and treasured electronic equipment! Yet a point may be reached at which it is best to seek help to get the bullying stopped. How should this be done? In part it will depend upon the severity of the bullying. It may be wise in extreme cases to involve the police. Much more likely, however, the victim of cyber bullying or the parents of such a person will consider getting the school to help.

The school may deny any responsibility on the grounds that the actions of the perpetrator(s) were undertaken from outside the school. However, if the school is prepared to help, there are reasons to think that the bullying can be stopped. It is very important to recognize that the student perpetrators involved in cases of cyber bullying are usually students who are involved in traditional forms of bullying directed toward the same victims at school.[2] The school can investigate the problem, as it manifests itself in the school, and often actually identify those involved. From then on, it is a matter of choosing a means of intervention that is most appropriate: not simply one that is considered appropriate for cyber bullying (there is no single appropriate method), but rather one that is best suited to dealing with the wider problem, that is, what has been happening between the students in question at school and beyond. The most appropriate method may turn out to be any one of the six methods we have examined, or a combination of them.

A major concern about the treatment of cases of cyber bullying is that the moral outrage that understandably takes place when cases of extreme forms of such bullying have come to light will lead people to believe that only a punitive response will suffice. The sheer novelty of this kind of bullying and its horrifying potential have fuelled this reaction. This has led to the demonizing of anybody who does anything that is offensive to anybody via the net or mobile phone, on the assumption that it is invariably a more harmful practice than face-to-face verbal abuse. Research shows, however, that most forms of cyber bullying are not regarded by schoolchildren as more hurtful than traditional bullying experienced at school.[3]

It is not uncommon to publicize extreme consequences that can be applied to those engaging in some forms of cyber bullying, with penalties of up to a maximum of 15 years in jail. Examples of such extreme treatments being meted out to students guilty of cyber bullying are generally unavailable; but it is sometimes felt that the announcement of the possibility of such extreme penalties may act as a deterrent and – given the growing menace – are justified. Unfortunately the existence of threats of extreme punishment that are not carried out become derisory and ineffective. Even the use of milder punishments may not always be the best way of dealing with the problem. Other ways need to be considered.

A case in point concerned a 16-year-old girl who had managed to get some exceedingly offensive statements about another girl's alleged sexual behavior posted on a site (www.whozadog.com) that had been created to enable people who are angry about someone or something supposedly to 'let off steam'. The victim and her father (who was incensed) had complained to the school and the offender and accomplice were duly identified. The father understandably wanted to take legal action against the perpetrator. The school counselor agreed that this might be done, but suggested that a nonpunitive approach might be considered. Eventually it was agreed that a mediational approach could be attempted as part of the Method of Shared Concern. It turned out to be successful and acceptable relations were reestablished between the two girls. In this case, the use of this method was made possible by the thoughtful and sensitive work undertaken by the counselor with the parents of the victim – and importantly with the support of the school principal.

I conclude that in many respects dealing with cases of cyber bullying, once those involved have been identified, is no different from dealing with traditional forms of bullying; that is, the school is challenged to choose and carry out the interventions they believe to be most appropriate.

An exercise

As an aid to discussing what choices may be made in the employment of a given method, readers may like to consider the following cases. Consider which one(s) may be most appropriately dealt with using the approaches described above. These are: (i) the traditional disciplinary approach, (ii) strengthening the victim, (iii) mediation, (iv) restorative practice, (v) the Support Group Method, and (vi) Method of Shared Concern. Bear in mind that more than one method may sometimes be applied in a particular case.

Case 1: An adolescent boy is found to have sexually assaulted a girl in the school playground.

Case 2: Several girls in secondary school have been identified as spreading rumors about another girl being a lesbian. She is very angry about it.

Case 3: A secondary schoolboy has been identified as continually upsetting another younger boy by taunting him about his father being in jail. When asked to reflect on what he has been doing the older boy feels ashamed of himself.

Case 4: Two young boys are continually arguing and upsetting each other at school. One of them has gained the ascendancy.

Case 5: A quiet, shy girl aged nine years is continually being ridiculed by some girls in her class. She has started staying away from school. She tells the teacher about how upset she is.

Case 6: A child keeps complaining that other students keep saying they do not like him.

Case 7: A child in kindergarten is continually going around attacking and hurting other children.

Case 8: Some girls keep ridiculing one of their mates because she is overweight.

Case 9: A teenage boy has viciously attacked another boy causing him serious injuries. The parents of the attacker are dismayed that their son should do such a thing. Legal action is pending, but an alternative course of action may be acceptable to the injured boy and parents of the victim.

Case 10: Abusive comments have been put on the Internet about the alleged sexual behavior of a 15-year-old girl. The culprit has been identified.

Case 11: Some girls have been constantly ridiculing a boy who has arrived at the school from an orphanage in Croatia, because he does not know who his father is.

Case 12: Nasty e-mails are being received by an adolescent boy ridiculing him on the grounds that he is gay. Inquiries at the school reveal that a group of boys are continually harassing the adolescent.

Case 13: Three black adolescents have been bullying a white student whom they allege has been making racist remarks about them.

Sources of Bias in the Choice of Method

After reading the suggested 'answers'[4] to the questions raised in the exercise, and having spoken to others about their answers, teachers will probably find that there are marked differences of opinion. Although we cannot hope to fully explain why individual teachers differ in their judgments, it may be useful to examine some of the factors that have been suggested to account for the differences. This will unavoidably involve categorizing people – always a dangerous thing to do – and attributing preferences for different kinds of actions to basic philosophies or orientations. Years ago Gilbert and Sullivan satirized this approach:

> *I often think it's comical – Fal, lal, la!*
> *How Nature always does contrive – Fal, lal, la!*
> *That every boy and every gal*

That's born into the world alive
Is either a little Liberal
Or else a little Conservative!
Fal, lal, la![5]

Dangerous though it may be to generalize about types of people, it does appear that basic and divergent moral orientations may underpin the judgments teachers among others make in deciding what they must do about undesirable behavior and bullying in particular. The two basic moral orientations are

1. the pursuit of justice and
2. the pursuit of care for others.

The pursuit of justice leads to the use of sanctions and punishment in accordance with the rules imposed by school authorities.[6] The pursuit of care for others leads to the use of problem-solving approaches to cases of bullying, such as mediation, the Support Group Method, and the Method of Shared Concern. According to some theorists, the pursuit of justice tends to be stronger in the male; the pursuit of care for others a female quality.[7] To the extent that a school staff is concerned with considerations of care rather than justice, nonpunitive methods of intervention appear to be more likely. I would argue that examining one's preferences for actions in the light of this understanding may be useful for some teachers. But the making of judgments about what to do with bullies and victims is certainly more complex than these philosophical or ideological categories suggest.

It turns out that whether to intervene at all in cases of bullying is predicted independently by *both* a justice orientation and a caring orientation on the part of teachers. Each acts as a spur to action, albeit often to rather different actions. And beyond these orientations are the judgments teachers make, based upon their appraisals of what is serious and what is not so serious. Not surprisingly, when teachers see bullying as relatively serious they are more likely to act.

What is serious is a question that divides teachers. For some teachers, spitting and swearing constitute a very serious transgression, while exclusion and nonverbal gestures directed at a target frequently, do not. Others disagree. Where there is a consensus on what constitutes serious bullying, a genuine 'whole school approach' becomes much more feasible.

A further difference among teachers is about the degree of empathy students feel for the victim of bullying.[8] This too has been shown to be a significant predictor of action to intervene. To some extent, the differences between teachers in degree of empathy may be constitutional. Empathy and helping behavior have been found to be sometimes motivated by personal sadness[9] and this may be evoked more readily in teachers who have actually experienced being bullied as children. Teachers who have themselves been bullied in childhood are more inclined than others to take action to prevent bullying from happening, by holding discussions with their classes.[10]

It has also been proposed that whether a teacher intervenes in a case of bullying is in part determined by a sense of self-efficacy, that is, the capacity to achieve desired goals. Whether this is the case when self-efficacy is conceived globally, that is, as applying in a wide range of goals, is unclear. But there is evidence that perceived self-efficacy in applying behavior management is a significant factor.[11] One would expect this capacity to be increased with appropriate teacher training.

Finally, the choice of method is (or should be) in part determined by how the alternative approaches have been evaluated.

Evaluating Interventions

The choice of method should be influenced largely, if not entirely, by results obtained from relevant research. As far as possible, the relevant research should be sought and evaluated. This requirement places considerable demands upon the school and especially on practitioners of intervention methods. Where little or no research is available, schools should evaluate the effectiveness of their own applications.

We often come across statements to the effect that a given mode of intervention is effective and is 'evidence-based'. Or that another approach is not evidence-based and is therefore invalid. Such claims need to be examined carefully, especially if they are based upon evidence collected by the promoter of the method!

The first question to be asked is: What exactly has been evaluated? Is it, for instance, an anti-bullying program with a variety of elements? If so, one may be able to say whether the program *as a whole* has had the intended effect but without knowing *which elements* have contributed significantly. Was it due to an improvement in surveillance perhaps, or due to classroom activities, or due to the work of peer supporters[12] and student bystanders, or due to a mode of intervention in cases of bullying, or due to the training of parents? One cannot tell. The level of bullying may have gone down without us knowing why. Despite studying the effectiveness of many anti-bullying programs, we are generally in the dark about what was the crucial component, or components, and whether the intervention method with actual cases made a significant impact.

This is not to say that the evaluation of programs with multiple elements is not worthwhile. A school may reasonably want to know whether *the total package* has worked. If so, the only reasonable way of finding out is to make use of valid research design of the kind that enables one to compare changes over a period when the program was implemented with changes that are likely to have occurred without the program being implemented. For instance, a pretest/posttest control group design may be used or an approximation to such a design.[13] However, finding a suitable 'control school' or better still 'control schools' for comparison purposes can be very difficult and beyond the resources of most schools. An acceptable alternative is to make comparisons between changes that occur in year groups over a period when an intervention program is actually implemented, and compare these with changes (if any) that occurred in the previous year with the same year groups over the same time period. This so-called age-cohort design is much easier to apply and has many advantages.

Inevitably, a decision to evaluate possible changes in levels or degrees raises the difficult question of how bullying is to be measured. Generally speaking, it is better and more practicable to make use of existing instruments that have been carefully developed and widely applied. Such instruments typically take the form of questionnaires that are answered anonymously by students in classrooms. They seek to provide reliable data on the extent to which students have experienced being bullied by peers and/or bullied others in different ways over a given time period.[14]

Scientific studies in the 'real world' cannot provide data of the same precision as that obtained in laboratory settings. But it is certainly no answer to our difficulties to say that we should not try, but instead simply listen to what school personnel say afterward in describing their impressions. At times there is a tendency to disparage attempts to undertake an objective analysis of the effectiveness of anti-bullying initiatives. For example, one writer on school bullying has opined that the issue of proof of effectiveness of methods is not one that should be of major concern. He asserts that pre- and post-program tests about the effectiveness of anti-bullying programs lack depth and meaning in the real world of the school'.[15] It is of course true that evaluations do not deliver 'proof'. They have limitations of which researchers are aware and do all they can to overcome. As an alternative to reliance on the subjective impressions of the practitioners of a method, carefully conceived empirical studies are surely to be encouraged.

The issue of evaluation that is most relevant to this book concerns whether given interventions to address *cases* of bullying are effective. Naturally in providing any answers to this question, we must specify the wider context in which the intervention took place and especially what else might have contributed to the intervention method being successful or unsuccessful. If we find that the method is generally successful when applied in a diversity of situations or with different kinds of bullying and with different age groups, we may conclude that the intervention method is indeed robust. On the other hand, it may be found that the method is successful with some groups and in some situations but not others. This too is useful information.

To date the typical or classical experimental research design appears to have been little used, if at all, in evaluating and comparing different kinds of interventions in cases of bullying. This is unfortunate as it would, for example, be of considerable interest in comparing outcomes for dealing with bully/victim problems using punitive and nonpunitive approaches. There is, however, work in progress as part of the KiVa anti-bullying program in Finland comparing these two different approaches as undertaken in different schools.[16] At the present time (December 2009), we eagerly await the Finnish report.

Within a school environment, allocating students involved in similar bully/victim problems to alternative treatments is generally impractical. Rules typically determine how similar cases are to be treated. However, there is no reason why schools should not systematically monitor and record outcomes after they have employed a particular intervention method. Unfortunately, this monitoring is seldom done in a way that yields useful data.

To obtain useful data, observations are required of the behavior of both the bullies and the victims who have been involved in a particular case, over a reasonable period of time, that is, before and after the intervention. In more extreme or severe cases, the monitoring process should be longer. Single subject research designs may be employed where it is deemed appropriate.[17] Such designs enable researchers to measure and monitor changes in the behavior of individual subjects over time. These may differ in complexity according to the measurements taken of student behavior and the frequency of assessments carried out. As a minimum, the practitioner would want to know whether the bullying has stopped, reduced, stayed the same, or actually increased in frequency and severity. This is not always easy to determine. Reliable reports are needed. The reporters must not be biased in any way. Ideally schools need multiple sources of information, for example, from those students involved in the bullying, peers, parents, and teachers. Any post-intervention interviews conducted with those involved in the bullying should be undertaken by a staff member or researcher not responsible for the application of the method, that is, a neutral person. Otherwise, the bully or bullies and victim may feel under pressure from the interviewer to provide the responses the practitioner wants to get. Experimenter bias has been observed in psychological studies[18] and can easily invalidate findings.

It has been argued in this book that the choice of method of intervention should be determined by the nature of the case of bullying. Each method appears to have its strengths and limitations. It is therefore of considerable importance in reporting results to specify the nature of the case to which the method was applied. Only in this way can generalizations emerge about the conditions in which particular kinds of interventions can be most effective. In addition, it should be made as clear as possible how the method was applied – variations to the method of intervention can be crucial.

The strength of the finding also needs to be evaluated. One would expect some cases to be resolved without an intervention, simply through the elapsing of time. Hence statistical considerations must apply. We must not be content in saying that four cases were dealt with and things got better every time. This can easily occur by chance. Just how overwhelming the positive changes must be before a valid claim can be made about the success of an intervention is a matter for persons with appropriate statistical knowledge to decide. It is often sensible for a school to employ the services of experienced evaluators, in some cases from university departments where individuals are particularly interested in this area of applied social research. This improves the credibility of claims.

Engaging an expert may raise a further problem, one that is currently frustrating valuable research in this field, namely, ethical determinations by relevant bodies. Often the permission granted to people from outside schools to do research is provided in such a way that it invalidates the research – for example, the requirement of parental approval prior to a student participating can at times practically decimate one's sample. This difficulty can be overcome by educational authorities recognizing the importance of evaluation studies and paving the way for unhampered research. Collaborative studies involving both school and university staff can sometimes overcome this problem.

Incorporating Intervention Strategy in a Whole School Policy

Evaluations are certainly not infallible. The evidence is rarely if ever completely compelling. However, at some point a school needs to agree to a decision about how cases of bullying are to be addressed.

And what is agreed is incorporated into a more general policy about what to do about bullying. Bear in mind that what has been called the reactive response to bullying forms one part only of the general strategy for tackling bullying in a school. As noted earlier, prevention is better than cure and whatever a school can do to promote positive behavior removes the need to discourage negative behavior. To the extent that preventative action is successful, the need for reactive action in cases of bullying will be lessened – and also made more practicable since there will be fewer cases to deal with. As many educators have observed, interventions work better when they form part of a well-designed comprehensive whole school approach.

Anti-bullying policies commonly assert that there will be 'consequences' for those who engage in bullying. It is sometimes not clear what is meant. To most people, and possibly all children, the promised consequences consist of something unpleasant – a penalty or a punishment. However, as used by many teachers, the word 'consequences' has much more general meaning and, some would say, at times a rather obscure meaning. Broadly, it stands for what will happen next; what will inevitably befall you. As applied to *some* of the methods, the meaning may be relatively clear. To the traditional disciplinarian it means some sort of punishment. To the practitioner of restorative practice it means authoritative pressure to experience remorse. But what can be said of the mediation approach that requires an uncoerced readiness to take part in negotiation and reach a peaceful settlement? We might be able to stretch language and usage far enough to apply the term 'consequences' to describe what is involved in the noncoercive processes that characterize the Support Group Method and the Method of Shared Concern, but only at the expense of using the term in an unfamiliar and (to some) confusing way. Is it better to drop the term or to try to explain to everyone what you mean by it? Does it mean, I wonder, anything more than this: We will not ignore any bullying and are determined that we will do something about it, something we consider appropriate.

There will inevitably be different opinions on what action is to be taken when children bully. One school may decide to use only disciplinary means in dealing with cases of bullying; another school may decide to rely exclusively on nonpunitive means. But whatever is decided, schools should be clear about the assumptions they are making in justifying their choice of method, and be prepared to change their approach if the evidence does not support its use. As suggested, some staff are likely to want to differentiate between those cases in which they think disciplinary action is required and other cases in which it is not required. This I think is a reasonable position to take. In fact, school anti-bullying policies commonly accommodate or permit both methods of intervention. For instance, they may approve the use of a mediation approach in relatively mild cases of bullying and punitive action in severe cases. They may recognize that a number of approaches may sometimes be used in a particular case.

A difficulty arises when a school policy begins with strong language denouncing bullying as 'unacceptable' or even (I have seen this) 'illegal' and as requiring 'zero tolerance'. Such language implies that one means business and seems to lead inevitably to the endorsement of a traditional disciplinary approach. This satisfies some people who believe schools are being too soft. But it produces dissonance when one reads further and discovers that the same school is actually advocating the use of mediation in some cases. The document will have a greater impact if its different parts are consistent – or if apparent inconsistencies can be reconciled. One may lose the immediate support of those who are angry and frustrated about schools not stopping the bullying by sticking to one kind of method of intervention. But in the long run, there is much to be said for the use of more temperate and realistic language in describing the school's position on dealing with bullying. It allows for flexibility and experiment.

Another problematic approach to dealing with cases of bullying lies in assuming that seeking the involvement of parents in *all* cases of bullying is necessary or desirable. Parents typically want to be involved. Some schools are anxious to secure parent support in addressing all cases of bullying. There are schools that announce through their anti-bullying policy that whenever bullying is observed, parents should be contacted and their involvement secured. With severe forms of bullying, and especially when a crime has been committed or a child seriously hurt, this makes sense. Schools however need to consider whether this is necessary in all cases of bullying. Under some circumstances of teasing and mild bullying, the school may see the matter as one that it can take care of – *in loco parentis.*

On occasions, schools have sought to place the responsibility for the solution of a problem of bullying on the parents of the children who are in conflict – that is, the parents of the bully and the parents of the targeted child – and to suggest that they meet to restore peace and harmony. This is almost always a mistake. The parents of the contending children typically defend the behavior of their children and accuse each other – and the others' child – of behaving unreasonably. This situation is well satirized in a play, *God of Carnage*,[19] which aims at exposing the myth that human beings can invariably negotiate their way, politely and reasonably, out of potential and real conflict. While conflict resolution can sometimes be practiced effectively, where one's own children are involved the chances of a successful outcome are close to zero.

As we have seen, where a range of methods of intervention is acceptable, school staff need to come to a general agreement on the circumstances under which each may be used. Practical guidelines are needed. Some schools have opted to provide flow charts that may help. A basic divergence between schools is whether one starts off with or ends up with a traditional disciplinary approach. It is sometimes proposed that nonpunitive approaches, such as mediation and the Method of Shared Concern, are undertaken when the punitive method has failed. This position, I think, should be reconsidered. It is extremely difficult for a nonpunitive approach to achieve success *after* the bullies or suspected bullies have been accused, tried, and punished. They almost always feel some degree of resentment and feel they cannot really trust the school when a practitioner of the nonpunitive approach takes over. It is generally better to use a disciplinary approach if – and only if – the nonpunitive method has not succeeded in stopping the bullying.

Should the children who have been targeted by a bully or bullies have a say in how their case is treated? Some schools have thought so. For the victim, this can be empowering. If the decision made by the victim is for the school to go to mediation or use a restorative practice instead of a punishment, the bully may well feel that the victim is the kind of person who does not hold a grudge and a win–win outcome is possible. On the other hand, the bully may view the decision made by the victim against punishment as an act of weakness – and continue to treat him or her with contempt.

A question naturally arises as to whether a school should spell out in detail what it intends to do when bullying occurs. Here one should distinguish between what it is useful for different readers of a school anti-bullying policy to know. For instance, teachers in a school may need instruction on what approaches for dealing with cases are acceptable, who should be informed, and what records are to be kept. They need to know when and how parents are to be involved. Certain people in the school may be designated to apply particular methods, especially if the methods are relatively complex and require special training for their application. If a method is unsuccessfully applied and the bullying continues, teachers need to know who is to be informed and what further action is required. These are matters for the internal working of a school and generally need not concern students or parents.

Undertaking to work out a plan and communicating it to a staff of teachers and counselors is no easy matter. In my experience of talking with numerous teachers at different schools and viewing anti-bullying policies, the crucial question of what to do with cases of bullying has scarcely been asked. It is unlikely that an absolute consensus on what to do will ever be completely achieved. But we do know that unless there is hard and careful thinking on this difficult issue – and the achievement of strong support for an agreed plan – little impact will be made on the serious and enduring problem of school bullying.

Endnotes

1   This comment was made by Ralph Waldo Emerson (1830–1882) the American essayist and poet. See Atkinson (1940).
2   The relationship between cyber bullying and traditional bullying (that is not using cyber technology) is explored in a report on a survey conducted with secondary school students in England by Smith *et al.* (2008).

3 See Smith *et al.* (2008) for an account of how students rate the harmfulness of cyber and non-cyber bullying.

4 For each of these cases, alternative courses of action may be justified, depending in part on the philosophy of the school, personal views of school staff, legal requirements, and relevant expertise available to the school. My own personal view would be that the disciplinary approach should seriously be considered in Cases 1, 9, and 10 (with community conferencing as a possibility). A less formal restorative practice appears justified in Case 3. In Case 7 a serious talk with the parents is needed, with possible sanctions if the behavior persists. For Case 4 a mediational approach would be appropriate. The problems experienced by the 'victims' in Cases 6 and 8 may be resolved through 'strengthening' the victim by social skills training, for example, by promoting greater assertiveness or employing a 'fogging' response. The Support Group Method or the Method of Shared Concern should be considered for Cases 2, 5, 11, and 12. Because there appears to have been some provocation in Case 13, the Method of Shared Concern might handle the matter more appropriately.

5 This satirical piece is sung by Private Willis in the Gilbert and Sullivan light opera *Iolanthe*, Act II.

6 Ellis and Shute (2007) found that, among Australian school teachers, care orientation predicted a problem-solving response to a hypothetical bullying situation, while a justice orientation predicted a rules–sanction response. In addition, the perceived seriousness of the bullying was a strong factor in determining whether teachers were prepared to intervene.

7 Carol Gilligan (1982) famously proposed this hypothesis, arguing that men and women tended to have different moral orientations, with men emphasizing considerations of justice and women a more caring approach to social problems.

8 Dedousis-Wallace and Shute (2009) have shown that high levels of overall empathy on the part of teachers can motivate action to intervene in cases of indirect bullying.

9 Fulz *et al.* (1988) argue that helping others is, in part, motivated by a desire to relieve personal sadness.

10 Kallestad and Olweus (2003) have reported that one of the factors predicting whether teachers work with classes to counter school bullying is having been personally bullied as a child.

11 The perceived self-efficacy of elementary school teachers in behavior management has been shown to predict the likelihood of teachers intervening in cases of bullying (Yoon 2004).

12 Bear in mind that 'peer support' can include a number of different activities, such as mediation, mentoring, befriending, and peer counseling (Naylor & Cowie 1999). Each one of these may have different effects on the prevalence of bullying in a school and the harm it can do.

13 Appropriate research designs for social inquiries are described in the now classical text provided by Campbell and Stanley (1963). For detailed discussions of research designs that are appropriate for assessing the effects of anti-bullying programs, see Olweus (2005) and Ttofi *et al.* (2008).

14 A widely used set of questionnaires designed to assess bullying in schools is contained in a package known as the Peer Relations Assessment Questionnaires (PRAQs). The package includes questionnaires and instructional manuals suitable for use with (i) senior students, (ii) junior students – using pictorial representations, (iii) teachers, and (iv) parents. They provide complementary estimates of the prevalence of bullying behavior in a school as well as information about student well-being and other related matters. See www.kenrigby.net and Rigby (2009). These questionnaires will be made available through ACER Press.

15 See the Foreword by Keith Sullivan (p. iv) to Robinson and Maines (2008).

16 The KiVa study is being undertaken in Finland by Salmivalli, Karna, and Poskiparta. In this study, teachers in half of the 78 intervention schools were encouraged to use strong disciplinary methods; in the rest of the intervention schools, teachers were encouraged to deal with bullying situations in a nonpunitive way. This information was provided by Ttofi *et al.* (2008).

17 See Barlow *et al.* (2007) for an examination of single subject research designs.

18 See Rosenthal (1966) for an examination of the problem of experimenter bias and steps that can be taken to minimize it.

19 The play, *The God of Carnage* (*Le Dieu du Carnage*) was written by Yasmina Reza (2006). It was first performed in Zurich in 2007.

Chapter 12

Backdrop and Beyond

There is a backdrop to every book. My study of bullying dating back to my first forays in 1989 has been accompanied by increasing skepticism. I have read widely and attended many conferences on school bullying. Many clever and wise things have been said. Many careful analyses of the problem have been presented. Thoughtful and considered plans have been announced. I have been heartened by the enthusiasm for the cause. Yet there is a great deal more work that must be done before we can confidently say how bullying can be addressed successfully.

I think all of us who began the journey 30 or so years ago will recall the burst of amazement that greeted the revelation that in Norway a certain Professor Dan Olweus had demonstrated that bullying could be reduced by as much as 50 percent if we only followed his lead. Well, many people did follow his lead and while papers continued to flow from Olweus et al. in Norway replicating the original findings, though less emphatically, other researchers were raising serious questions about why the program was not working elsewhere in the same way.

Bullying Interventions in Schools: Six Basic Approaches, First Edition. Ken Rigby.
© 2012 Ken Rigby. Published 2012 by Blackwell Publishing Ltd.

Nothing daunted, more and more educators devised new programs to reduce bullying, often claiming significant success. All of them took on board one of the key messages from Olweus that the approach to stopping bullying must be a 'whole school' approach. Not just a few teachers, but the whole staff; not only the staff but the student body; not only these, but parents as well. The whole enterprise must be coordinated. No one could argue against this.

Especially, it has been said, we must strive to produce an environment in which no one was motivated to bully. This implied that we must do everything we can to establish positive relationships – between children and their peers, between teachers and their students, between teachers and teachers, between teachers and parents. Methods were duly devised and promoted to raise the empathy level of all children, to promote friendly and helpful interactions between children, to educate children in classrooms about the evil of bullying, to promote assertiveness and train suitable children to become peer supporters, and to ensure that there was adequate surveillance in the school playground in case things did not work out. And to intervene – if really necessary.

In the first decade of the twenty-first century, there has been a wave of evaluative studies to determine how effective these initiatives have been. As we have seen, they make very sobering reading. The progress toward eliminating bullying in schools has been modest at best; some evaluators have opined that nothing can be said to have worked.

That then is the backdrop to the book.

It is surely time for reappraisal. It is tempting to conclude that countering bullying in schools is a futile enterprise. Original sin will always beat us. Or, if we disavow theological explanations, our primeval impulses will always get the better of us. Is it as bad as that? Well, no. The secular world closes in upon me and dispels my pessimism. If we look again at the documented history of systematic interventions to stop school bullying, we can see glimmerings of hope. In a number of countries there have been reports of a diminution of bullying over time. Some progress is being reported, especially in schools where the implementation of programs has been thorough.[1] Even researchers who have reported a general lack of success have noted that *some* schools have been successful in reducing bullying.[2]

It is all very well, the cynic in me says, to go on about the virtue of 'a whole school approach' and how success will be achieved if we thoroughly implement what we know. But the question remains: implementing what? Are all efforts to address bullying equally worthy?

My deep concern is that there has been little evaluation of the effectiveness of specific elements of anti-bullying programs. Whenever possible in this book I have sought to provide relevant evidence. But it is sparse. In some cases it appears contradictory or inconclusive. On the surface, one may be forgiven for believing that there is consensus. Indeed there is a level of agreement: that we should all pull together using the whole school approach; that we should do what we can to promote more positive relations; that we should undertake interventions *thoroughly*. Beneath the surface things are different. Listen to teachers talk about what they think they should be doing about bullying. Read what the experts have to say and see how they contradict one another.

Currently the loudest voices are from those who are putting all, or nearly all, of their eggs in one basket – we may call this the preventative approach. To many people this is a refreshing change from the view that we should wait until bullying happens and nab them. Prevention – if we know how to prevent successfully – is certainly better than cure, and we must continue working on how we can improve the social climate of schools so as to discourage bullying. To some extent, this prioritizing of prevention is an understandable reaction to the traditional disciplinary approach, a commonly unsuccessful way of dealing with cases. But has the pendulum swung too far? It is the subtext of this book that it has.

As I have tried to show, punishment, the central feature of the traditional and still widely supported approach, often does not work (though at times it may be seen as necessary) and can in fact be counterproductive. What is, as yet, not fully realized is that there is now a range of alternative treatments or interventions that can, under some circumstances, actually work. I have tried to explain each of these methods and to identify the strengths and limitations of each. What I believe we need to do is to determine just how these methods can work in practice in the school environment.

Mild though this proposal is, I have no doubt that it will meet with some opposition, not only from those who think that I am denying the importance of preventive strategies (I am not) but also from those who have a fixed and cherished view as to how one *must* proceed when a student has been discovered bullying someone. The main proposal of this book is in a sense simple: understand and appreciate what the alternative approaches are, and ask, on balance, which one shall I use in *this* case; the one that is now before me.

I was asked recently at a workshop whether I had any reservations about restorative practice. I replied that indeed I had (the true believer winced) and that I had reservations about all the others as well. But this is not a call for inaction – far from it. It is rather a call for us to think through all of the methods before we commit ourselves to act.

I suspect that my skepticism and misgivings about any one method being the *only one* acceptable is painful to some – whether it be the traditional disciplinary method, strengthening the victim, mediation, restorative practice, the Support Group Method, or the Method of Shared Concern. It can be very hard to keep an open mind until the facts of the case emerge and the pros and cons of each option have been weighed. It can be unsettling to question the current orthodoxy or review the evidence for the method to which one has become committed. Five centuries ago, the first modern political thinker told us this and predicted heavy weather for the innovator:

> And it ought to be remembered that there is nothing more difficult to take in hand, more perilous to conduct, or more uncertain in its success, than to take the lead in the introduction of a new order of things. Because the innovator has for enemies all those who have done well under the old conditions, and lukewarm defenders in those who may do well under the new. This coolness arises partly from fear of the opponents, who have the laws on their side, and partly from the incredulity of men, who do not readily believe in new things until they have had a long experience of them.[3]

Endnotes

1 Hanewinkel (2004) carried out a large-scale intervention in schools in Germany in the 1990s, based in part on the Olweus model. Overall there were no significant reductions in bullying, but some schools reported that victimization diminished significantly.

2 According to Salmivalli *et al.* (2004), when schools consistently and rigorously implement an anti-bullying policy the outcomes can be very positive with over 50 percent reductions recorded in some Finnish schools.

3 This piece of political insight comes from Machiavelli's classical book, *The Prince*, Chapter VI, published originally in 1515. The quotation is taken from the translation by W. K. Marriott in 1908 and published in paperback in 2008.

Appendix A

Handling Bullying Questionnaire with Results

Teachers have alternative ways of dealing with incidents of bullying in a school. To some extent, what is done depends on the circumstances in which the bullying takes place, and the severity of the bullying. It is, of course, sometimes difficult to generalize, but in answering the following questions, indicate what you think you **might** do.

Imagine the following scenario:

> A 12-year-old student is being repeatedly teased and called unpleasant names by another, more powerful, student who has successfully persuaded other students to avoid the targeted person as much as possible. As a result, the victim of this behavior is feeling angry, miserable, and often isolated.

Percentages of US teachers and counselors (N=735) responding to each suggested way of acting:

Bullying Interventions in Schools: Six Basic Approaches, First Edition. Ken Rigby.
© 2012 Ken Rigby. Published 2012 by Blackwell Publishing Ltd.

	I definitely would	I probably would	I am unsure	I probably would not	I definitely would not
1. I would insist that the bully 'cut it out'	65	18	5	8	5
2. I would treat the matter lightly	1	1	2	18	78
3. I would make sure the bully was suitably punished	38	33	17	7	2
4. I would discuss the matter with my colleagues at school	56	33	4	4	1
5. I would convene a meeting of students, including the bully or bullies, tell them what was happening, and ask them to suggest ways they could help improve the situation	24	31	20	18	6
6. I would tell the victim to stand up to the bully	11	25	24	29	11
7. I would make it clear to the bully that his or her behavior would not be tolerated	83	14	1	1	1

(Continued)

	I definitely would	I probably would	I am unsure	I probably would not	I definitely would not
8. I would leave it for someone else to sort out	1	1	4	25	67
9. I would share my concern with the bully about what happened to the victim, and seek to get the bully to behave in a more caring and responsible manner	42	37	10	8	2
10. I would let the students sort it out themselves	1	2	3	34	57
11. I would suggest that the victim act more assertively	18	41	18	17	5
12. I would discuss with the bully options from which he or she could make a choice in order to improve the situation	39	43	9	5	2
13. I would ask the school counselor to intervene	61	24	7	2	1

	I definitely would	I probably would	I am unsure	I probably would not	I definitely would not
14. I would refer the matter to an administrator (e.g., principal, vice-principal, dean)	43	31	17	7	1
15. I would contact the victim's parents or guardians to express my concern about their child's well-being	26	30	28	13	2
16. I would just tell the kids to 'grow up'	<.5	3	2	17	77
17. I would encourage the victim to show that he or she could not be intimidated	15	38	22	16	8
18. I would ignore it	2	<.5	1	8	87
19. I would help the bully achieve greater self-esteem so that he or she would no longer want to bully anyone	18	37	22	16	7

(*Continued*)

	I definitely would	I probably would	I am unsure	I probably would not	I definitely would not
20. I would insist to the parents(s) or guardian(s) of the bully that the behavior must stop	26	34	22	14	3
21. I would find the bully something more interesting to do	9	23	31	29	6
22. I would advise the victim to tell the bully to 'back off'	8	26	25	28	11

Note: Due to rounding off the percentage figures for each response category, not all totals add up to 100 percent. Reproduced with permission from Dr Ken Rigby, University of South Australia, and Dr Sheri Bauman, University of Arizona.

Appendix B

Exercise on Fogging

This exercise can be used at a meeting or workshop where people (teachers or students) are interested in role playing how 'fogging' might work.

Bully: You have a great big nose.
Target: *True, it is large.*
Bully: It looks like a beak.
Target: *True, it does stand out.*
Bully: You are the ugliest kid in the school.
Target: *That's your opinion.*
Bully: You are wearing pov shoes.
Target: *You are not wrong.*
Bully: You must be stupid to keep agreeing with me.
Target: *That's true.*
Bully: You keep saying that's true.
Target: *That's true.*

Bullying Interventions in Schools: Six Basic Approaches, First Edition. Ken Rigby.
© 2012 Ken Rigby. Published 2012 by Blackwell Publishing Ltd.

In the next part of this exercise the target replies by asking a question that can surprise and put the bully on the 'back foot'. The target simply looks at the bully with mild curiosity.

Bully: You are such an idiot.
Target: *Why do you think so? (Wait for the answer.)*
Bully: Everybody hates you.
Target: *That's interesting. Why do you think that? (Wait.)*
Bully: You are always in the library at lunch time.
Target: *That's right. Why does that concern you? (Wait.)*

Finally:

Bully: All those kids in the library are nerds.
Target: *It may seem like that to you.*
Bully: You have no friends.
Target: *That's what you think!*

Following this exercise, discuss how responding in this way – with supportive body language – could help, and discuss and devise possible responses that could be useful and acceptable to the target.

References

Allport, F.H. (1924) *Social Psychology*. Houghton Mifflin, Boston, MA.

Andershed, H., Kerr, M. & Stattin, H. (2001) Bullying in school and violence on the streets: Are the same people involved? *Journal of Scandinavian Studies on Crime and Crime Prevention*, 2, 31–49.

Atkinson, B. (ed.) (1940) *The Complete Essays and Other Writings of Ralph Waldo Emerson*. Random House, New York.

Baldry, A.C. & Farrington, D.P. (2007) Effectiveness of programs to prevent bullying. *Victims and Offenders*, 22, 183–204.

Ball, H.A., Arseneault, L., Taylor, A., Maughan, B., Caspi, A. & Moffatt, T.E. (2008) Genetic and environmental influences on victims, bullies and bully-victims. *Journal of Child Psychology and Psychiatry and Associated Disciplines*, 49, 104–112.

Barlow, D.H., Andrasik, F. & Hersen, M. (2007) *Single Case Experimental Design*. Allyn & Bacon, Boston, MA.

Bauman, S., Rigby, K. & Hoppa, K. (2008) US teachers' and school counsellors' strategies for handling school bullying incidents. *Educational Psychology*, 28, 837–856.

Bellhouse, B. (2009) *Beginner's Guide to Circle Time with Primary School Students*. Inyahead Press, Sydney, New South Wales, Australia.

Bullying Interventions in Schools: Six Basic Approaches, First Edition. Ken Rigby.
© 2012 Ken Rigby. Published 2012 by Blackwell Publishing Ltd.

Blood, P. & Thorsborne, M. (2006, October) Overcoming resistance to wholeschool uptake of restorative practices. Paper presented at the *International Institute of Restorative Practices. The Next Step: Developing Restorative Communities, Part 2*, Bethlehem, PA.

Bond, L., Carlin, J.B., Thomas, L., Ruin, K. & Patton, G. (2000) Does bullying cause emotional problems? A prospective study of young teenagers. *British Medical Journal*, 323, 480–484.

Braithwaite, J. (1989) *Crime, Shame and Reintegration*. Cambridge University Press, Cambridge, U.K.

Brown University Child and Adolescent Behavior Letter, The. (2002) Bullying prevention program may reduce aggression. (What's new in research). (Brief Article), 18, No. 12.

Burgess, A. (1962) *A Clockwork Orange*. Heinemann, London.

Campbell, D.T. & Stanley, J.C. (1963) *Experimental and Quasiexperimental Designs for Research*. Rand McNally, Chicago, IL.

Chesterton, G.K. (1915) *Tremendous Trifles*. Dodd, Mead & Company, New York.

Cohen, R. (2005) *Students Resolving Conflict: Peer Mediation in Schools*. Good Year Books, Tucson, AZ.

Cowie, H., Smith, P.K., Boulton, M. & Laver, R. (1994) *Cooperation in the Multiethnic Classroom*. David Fulton, London.

Cremin, H. (2002) Pupils resolving disputes: Successful peer mediation schemes share their secrets. *Support for Learning*, 17, 138–143.

Curwin, R. (1995) A humane approach to reducing violence in schools. *Educational Leadership*, 52, 72–75.

Dedousis-Wallace, A. & Shute, R. (2009) Indirect bullying: Predictors of teacher intervention, and outcome of a pilot educational presentation about impact on adolescent mental health. *Australian Journal of Educational & Developmental Psychology*, 9, 2–17.

Drewery, W. (2004) Conferencing in schools: Punishment, restorative justice and the productive importance of the process of conversation. *Journal of Community and Applied Social Psychology*, 14, 332–344.

Dubin, N. (2007) *Asperger Syndrome and Bullying: Strategies and Solutions*. Jessica Kingsley, London.

Duncan, A. (1996) The shared concern method for resolving group bullying in schools. *Educational Psychology in Practice*, 12 (2), 94–98.

Egan, S.K. & Perry, D.G. (1998) Does low self-regard invite victimization? *Developmental Psychology*, 34 (2), 299–309.

Ellis, A. (1961) *A Guide to Rational Living*. Prentice-Hall, Englewood Cliffs, NJ.

Ellis, A.A. & Shute, R. (2007) Teacher responses to bullying in relation to moral orientation and seriousness of bullying. *British Journal of Educational Psychology*, 77, 649–663.

Endressen, I.M. & Olweus, D. (2005) Participation in power sports and anti-social involvement in preadolescent and adolescent boys. *Journal of Child Psychology and Psychiatry*, 46, 468–478.

Erceg, E. & Cross, D. (2004) *Friendly Schools and Families: Teaching and Learning Handbook*. ACER Press, Camberwell, Victoria, Australia.

Farrington, D.P. (1993) Understanding and preventing bullying. In: *Crime and justice* (eds M. Tonny & N. Morris), Vol. 17. University of Chicago Press, Chicago, IL.

Ferguson, C.J., San Miguel, C., Kilburn, J.C. & Sanchez, P. (2007) The effectiveness of school-based anti-bullying programs: A meta-analytic review. *Criminal Justice Review*, 32, 401–414.

Ferris, K. (2003) Achieving a cultural revolution (1). *ServiceTalk – The Journal of the IT Service Management Forum*, 2.

Festinger, L. (1957) *A Theory of Cognitive Dissonance*. Stanford University Press, Stanford, CA.

Field, E.M. (1999) *Bully Busting*. Finch Publishing, Lane Cove, New South Wales, Australia.

Fulz, J., Schaller, M. & Cialdini, R.B. (1988) Empathy, sadness, and distress: Three related but distinct vicarious affective responses to another's suffering. *Personality and Social Psychology Bulletin*, 14, 312–325.

Garrity, C., Jens, K., Porter, W.P., Sager, N. & Short-Camilli, C. (1996) *Bullyproofing Your School*. Sopris West, Longmont, CO.

Gilligan, C. (1982) *In a Different Voice: Psychological Theory and Women's Development*. Harvard University Press, Cambridge, MA.

Gilligan, J. (1996) *Violence: Our Deadly Epidemic and Its Causes*. Grossett/Putnam Books, New York.

Goleman, D. (1995) *Emotional Intelligence*. Bantam Books, New York.

Goleman, D. (2006/2007) What is social intelligence? *Greater Good*, 111 (2), 44.

Griffiths, C. (2001) *Countering Bullying in Schools Training Package*. Western Australian Department of Education, Perth, WA.

Haber, J. (2007) *Bullyproof Your Child for Life*. Perigee, New York.

Hanewinkel, R. (2004) Prevention of bullying in German schools: An evaluation of an anti-bullying approach. In: *Bullying in Schools: How Successful Can Interventions Be?* (eds P.K. Smith, D. Pepler & K. Rigby), pp. 81–98. Cambridge University Press, Cambridge, MA.

Hawker, D.J. & Boulton, M.J. (2000) Twenty years' research on peer victimization and psychosocial maladjustment: A meta-analytic review of cross-sectional studies. *Journal of Child Psychology and Psychiatry*, 42, 441–455.

Houlston, C. & Smith, P.K. (2009) The impact of a peer counselling scheme to address bullying in an all-girl London secondary school: A short-term longitudinal study. *British Journal of Educational Psychology*, 79, 69–86.

Johnson, D. & Johnson, R. (1996) Effectiveness of conflict managers in an inner city elementary school. *Journal of Educational Research*, 98, 280–285.

Johnson, D.W., Johnson, R.T. & Dudley, B. (1992) Effects of peer mediation training on elementary school students. *Mediation Quarterly*, 10 (1), 89–99.

Johnson, D.W., Johnson, R.T. & Taylor, B. (1993) Impact of cooperative and individualistic learning on high-ability students' achievement, self esteem, and social acceptance. *Journal of Social Psychology*, 133 (6), 839–844.

Jourard, S.M. (1964) *The Transparent Self: Selfdisclosure and Wellbeing.* Van Nostrand Reinhold, New York.

Kallestad, K.J. & Olweus, D. (2003) Predicting teachers' and schools' implementation of the Olweus Bullying Prevention Program: A multilevel study. *Prevention & Treatment*, 6 (1), 21.

Kelman, H.C. (1961) Processes of opinion change. *Public Opinion Quarterly*, 25, 57–78.

King, K.A., Vidourek, R.A., Davis, B. & McClellan, W. (2002) Increasing self-esteem and school connectedness through a multidimensional mentoring program. *Journal of School Health*, 72, 294–299.

Kowalski, R., Limber, S. & Agatson, P. (2007) *Cyber Bullying.* Blackwell, Oxford, U.K.

Lewers, R. & Murphy, E. (2000) *The Hidden Hurt.* Wizard Books, Ballarat, Victoria, Australia.

Logan, G.M. & Adams, R.M. (Eds.) (2002) *More: Utopia.* Cambridge University Press, Cambridge, MA.

McGrath, H. & Noble, T. (2003) *BOUNCE BACK! A Classroom Resiliency Program.* Pearson Education, Sydney, New South Wales, Australia.

McGrath, H. & Noble, T. (2006) *Bullying Solutions: Evidencebased Approaches to Bullying in Australian Schools.* Pearson Books, Sydney, New South Wales, Australia.

Mahdavi, J. & Smith, P.K. (2002) The operation of a bully court and perceptions of its success: A case study. *School Psychology International*, 23, 327–341.

Marriott, W.K. (1908, 1998) *Machiavelli's the Prince.* Sterling Publishing Company, New York.

Menesini, E., Codecasa, E., Benelli, B. & Cowie, H. (2003) Enhancing children's responsibility to take action against bullying: Evaluation of a befriending intervention in Italian middle schools, *Aggressive Behaviour,* 29, 1–14.

Metzler, C.W., Biglan, A., Rusby, J.C. & Sprague, J.R. (2001) Evaluation of a comprehensive behavior management program to improve school-wide positive behavior support. *Education and Treatment of Children,* 24, 448–479.

Mishna, C. (2008) An overview of the evidence on bullying prevention and intervention programs. *Brief Treatment and Crisis Intervention,* 8, 327–341.

Molcho, M., Craig, W., Due, P., *et al.* (2009) Cross-national time trends in bullying behaviour 1994–2006: Findings from Europe and North America. *International Journal of Public Health,* 54 (2), 225–234.

Mosley, J. & Tew, M. (1999) *Quality Circle Time in the Secondary School – A Handbook of Good Practice.* David Fulton Publishers, London, U.K.

Naylor, P. & Cowie, H. (1999) The effectiveness of peer support systems in challenging school bullying: The perspectives and experiences of teachers and pupils. *Journal of Adolescence,* 22, 467–479.

Nettelbeck, T. & Wilson, C. (2002) Personal vulnerability to victimization of people with mental retardation. *Trauma, Violence, & Abuse,* 3, 289–306.

O'Connell, T., Wachtel, B. & Wachtel, T. (1999) *Conferencing Handbook: The New Real Justice Training Manual.* Piper's Press, Pipersville, PA.

O'Connor, M., Foch, T., Todd, S. & Plomin, R. (1980) A twin study of specific behavioural problems of socialisation as viewed by parents. *Journal of Abnormal Child Psychology,* 8, 189–199.

Olweus, D. (1993) *Bullying at School.* Blackwell, Cambridge, MA.

Olweus, D. (2005) A useful evaluation design, and effects of the Olweus Bullying Prevention Program. *Psychology, Crime & Law,* 11, 389–402.

Pellegrini, A.D. (2004) Bullying during middle school years. In: *Bullying: Implications for the Classroom* (eds C.E. Sanders & G.D. Pyne), pp. 177–199. Elsevier Academic Press, New York.

Pepler, D.J. & Craig, W.M. (1995) A peek behind the fence: Naturalistic observations of aggressive children with remote audiovisual recording. *Developmental Psychology,* 31, 545–553.

Pepler, D., Jiang, D., Craig, W. & Connolly, J. (2008) Developmental trajectories of bullying and associated factors. *Child Development*, 79, 325–338.

Pikas, A. (1989) The common concern method for the treatment of mobbing. In: *Bullying: An International Perspective* (eds E. Roland & E. Munthe). Fulton, London, U.K.

Pikas, A. (2002) New developments of the Shared Concern Method. *School Psychology International*, 23 (3), 307–336.

Readymade Productions (2007) *The Method of Shared Concern* (a staff training resource for dealing with bullying in schools). Adelaide, Readymade Productions. www.readymade.com.au/method

Renn, S., Van Velsen, J., Matheison, P., Dennis, K. & Langley, J. (2009). *The Bullying Intervention Toolkit*. Inyahead Press, Queenscliff, Victoria, Australia.

Reza, Y. (2006) *The God of Carnage: A Play* (*Le Dieu du Carnage*, translated by Christopher Hampton). Faber & Faber, London, U.K.

Rigby, K. (1996) *Bullying in Schools and What to Do About It*. ACER Press, Melbourne, Victoria, Australia.

Rigby, K. (1997a) Attitudes and beliefs about bullying among Australian school children. *Irish Journal of Psychology*, 18 (2), 202–220.

Rigby, K. (1997b) *Manual for the Peer Relations Questionnaire (PRQ)*. The Professional Reading Guide, Point Lonsdale, Victoria, Australia.

Rigby, K. (1998) The relationship between reported health and involvement in bully/victim problems among male and female secondary school students. *Journal of Health Psychology*, 4, 465–476.

Rigby, K. (2001) *Stop the Bullying*. ACER Press, Camberwell, Victoria, Australia.

Rigby, K. (2002a) *A Metaevaluation of Methods and Approaches to Reducing Bullying in Preschools and in Early Primary School in Australia*. Attorney-General's Department, Canberra, Australian Capital Territory, Australia.

Rigby, K. (2002b) *New Perspectives on Bullying*. Jessica Kingsley, London, U.K.

Rigby, K. (2003) Consequences of bullying in schools. *The Canadian Journal of Psychiatry*, 48, 583–590.

Rigby, K. (2005a) Bullying in schools and the mental health of children. *Australian Journal of Guidance and Counselling*, 15, 195–208.

Rigby, K. (2005b) The Method of Shared Concern as an intervention technique to address bullying in schools: An overview and appraisal. *Australian Journal of Counselling and Guidance*, 15, 27–34.

Rigby, K. (2008) *Children and Bullying: How Parents and Educators Can Reduce Bullying at School.* Wiley-Blackwell, Boston, MA.

Rigby, K. (2010, in press) *The Peer Relations Assessment Questionnaires (PRAQs).* ACER Press, Camberwell, Victoria, Australia.

Rigby, K. & Bagshaw, D. (2001) What hurts? The reported consequences of negative interactions with peers among Australian school children. *Children Australia,* 26 (4), 36–41.

Rigby, K. & Bagshaw, D. (2003) Prospects of adolescent students collaborating with teachers in addressing issues of bullying and conflict in schools. *Educational Psychology,* 32, 535–546.

Rigby, K. & Barnes, A. (2002) To tell or not to tell: The victimised student's dilemma. *Youth Studies, Australia,* 21 (3), 33–36.

Rigby, K. & Bauman, S. (2007) What teachers think should be done about cases of bullying. *Professional Educator.* ACER Press, Camberwell, Victoria, Australia.

Rigby, K. & Griffiths, C. (2010) *Applying the Method of Shared Concern in Australian Schools: An Evaluative Study.* Department of Education, Employment and Workplace Relations, Canberra, Australian Capital Territory, Australia.

Rigby, K. & Johnson, B. (2006) Expressed readiness of Australian school children to act as bystanders in support of children who are being bullied. *Educational Psychology,* 26, 425–441.

Rigby, K. & Sharp, S. (1993) Cultivating the art of self-defence among victimized children. *International Journal of Protective Behaviours,* 1 (2), 24–27.

Rigby, K. & Slee, P.T. (1993) Dimensions of interpersonal relating among Australian school children and their implications for psychological well-being. *Journal of Social Psychology,* 133, 447–456.

Rigby, K. & Slee, P.T. (1999) Involvement in bully/victim problems and perceived low social support. *Suicide and Lifethreatening Behavior,* 29, 119–30.

Rigby, K. & Slee, P.T. (2008) Interventions to reduce bullying. *International Journal of Adolescent Medicine and Health,* 20, 165–183.

Rigby, K. & Thomas, E.B. (2003) *How Schools Counter Bullying: Policies and Procedures in Selected Australian Schools.* The Professional Reading Guide, Point Lonsdale, Victoria, Australia.

Rigby, K., Schofield, P. & Slee, P.T. (1987) The similarity of attitudes to personal and impersonal types of authority among adolescent schoolchildren. *Journal of Adolescence,* 10, 241–253.

Rigby, K., Cox, I.K. & Black, G. (1997) Cooperativeness and bully/victim problems among Australian schoolchildren. *Journal of Social Psychology*, 137 (3), 357–368.

Robinson, G. & Maines, B. (1997) *Crying for Help: The No Blame Approach to Bullying*. Lucky Duck Publishing, Bristol, U.K.

Robinson, G. & Maines, B. (2008) *Bullying: A Complete Guide to the Support Group Method*. Sage, London, U.K.

Roland, E. & Galloway, D. (2002) Classroom influences on bullying. *Educational Research*, 44, 299–312.

Ronning, J.A., Sourander, A., Kumpulainen, K., *et al.* (2009) Cross-informant agreement about bullying and victimization among eight year olds: Whose information best predicts psychiatric caseness 10–15 years later? *Social Psychiatry & Psychiatric Epidemiology*, 44 (1), 15–22.

Rosenthal, R. (1966) *Experimenter Effects in Behavioral Research*. Appleton-Century-Crofts, New York.

Salmivalli, C., Kuukianen, A., Voetin, M. & Sinisammal, M. (2004) Targeting the group as a whole: The Finnish anti-bullying intervention. In: *Bullying in Schools: How Successful Can Interventions Be?* (eds P.K. Smith, D. Pepler & K. Rigby), pp. 251–274. Cambridge University Press, Cambridge, MA.

Seals, D. & Young, J. (2003) Bullying and victimization: Prevalence and relationship to gender, grade level, ethnicity, self esteem and depression. *Adolescence*, 38, 735–747.

Shariff, S. (2008) *Cyberbullying: Issues and Solutions for the School, the Classroom and the Home*. Routledge, New York.

Sherman, L.W. & Strang, H. (2007) *Restorative Justice: The Evidence*. The Smith Institute, London, U.K.

Siobhan, M. & Smith, P.K. (1995) Bullying and the child who stammers. *British Journal of Special Education*, 22, 24–27.

Skinner, B.F. (1953) *Science and Human Behavior*. Macmillan, New York.

Smith, P.K. (2001) Should we blame the bullies? *The Psychologist*, 14 (2), 61.

Smith, P.K. & Sharp, S. (Eds.) (1994) *School Bullying: Insights and Perspectives*. Routledge, London, U.K.

Smith, P.K., Pepler, D. & Rigby, K. (Eds.) (2004a) *Bullying in Schools: How Successful Can Interventions Be?* Cambridge University Press, Cambridge, MA.

Smith, P.K., Sharp, S., Eslea, M. & Thompson, D. (2004b) England: The Sheffield project. In: *Bullying in Schools: How Successful Can Interventions Be?* (eds P. K. Smith, D. Pepler & K. Rigby). Cambridge University Press, Cambridge, MA.

Smith, J.D., Schneider, B., Smith, P.K. & Ananiadou, K. (2004c) The effectiveness of whole-school antibullying programs: A synthesis of evaluation research. *School Psychology Review*, 33, 547–560.

Smith, P.K., Howard, S. & Thompson, F. (2007) Use of the Support Group Method to tackle bullying, and evaluation from schools and local authorities in England. *Pastoral Care in Education*, 25, 4–13.

Smith, P.K., Mahdavi, J., Carvalho, M., Fisher, S., Russell, S. & Tippett, N. (2008) Cyberbullying: Its nature and impact in secondary school pupils. *Journal of Child Psychology and Psychiatry*, 49, 376–385.

Solberg, M.E., Olweus, D. & Endressen, I.M. (2007) Bullies and victims at school: Are they the same pupils? *British Journal of Educational Psychology*, 77, 441–464.

Stevens, V., de Bourdeaudhuij, I. & Van Oost, P. (2000) Bullying in Flemish schools: An evaluation of anti-bullying intervention in primary and secondary schools. *British Journal of Educational Psychology*, 70, 195–210.

Storr, A. (1989) *Churchill's Black Dog and Other Phenomena of the Human Mind*. Fontana Collins, London, U.K.

Sullivan, K. (2000) *The Antibullying Handbook*. Oxford University Press, Oxford, U.K.

Sullivan, D. & Tifft, L. (2006) Introduction: The healing dimensions of restorative justice: A critical appraisal: A one-world body. In: *Handbook of Restorative justice*(eds D. Sullivan & L. Tifft). London: Routledge.

Sutton, J. & Keogh, E. (2001) Components of Machiavellian beliefs in children: Relationships with personality. *Personality and Individual Differences*, 30, 137–148.

Theberge, S. & Karan, O.C. (2004) Six factors inhibiting the use of peer mediation in a junior high school. *Professional School Counselling*, 7, 283–291.

Thorsborne, M. & Vinegrad, D. (2006) *Restorative Practice and the Management of Bullying: Rethinking Behaviour Management*. Inyahead Press, Queenscliff, Victoria, Australia.

Tremblay, E., Nagin, D.S., Sequin, J.R., *et al.* (2004) Physical aggression during early childhood: Trajectories and Predictors. *Pediatrics*, 114, 43–50.

Ttofi, M.M., Farrington, D.P. & Baldry, A.C. (2008) *Effectiveness of Programmes to Reduce School Bullying: A Systematic Review*. Swedish Council for Crime Prevention, Information and Publications, Stockholm, Sweden.

Vreeman, R.C. & Carroll, A.E. (2007) A systematic review of school-based interventions to prevent bullying. *Archives of Pediatrics and Adolescent Medicine*, 161, 78–88.

Whitted, K.S. & Dupper, D.R. (2005) Best practices for preventing or reducing bullying in schools. *Children & Schools*, 27 (3), 167–175.

Ykema, F. (2002) *The Rock and Water Perspective: Skills for Psychosocial Teaching with boys*. SWP, Amsterdam, the Netherlands.

Yoon, J.S. (2004) Predicting teacher intervention in bullying situations. *Education and Treatment of Children*, 27, 37–45.

Young, S. (1998) The Support Group Approach to bullying in schools. *Educational Psychology in Practice*, 14, 32–39.

Young, S. & Holdorf, G. (2003) Using solution focussed brief therapy in individual referrals for bullying. *Educational Psychology in Practice*, 19, 271–282.

Youth Justice Board, United Kingdom (2004) *National Evaluation of the Restorative Justice in Schools Programme*. Youth Justice Board, London, U.K. http://www.yjb.gov.uk/Publications/Resources/Downloads/nat%20ev%20of%20rj%20in%20schoolsfullfv.pdf

Index

Bullying Interventions in Schools: Six Basic Approaches, First Edition. Ken Rigby.
© 2012 Ken Rigby. Published 2012 by Blackwell Publishing Ltd.

162

Index